ro
ro
ro

Stefanie Schulz
Daniel Quinlan

See you –
im nächsten Sommer ✈

Eine deutsch-englische Geschichte

Rowohlt Taschenbuch Verlag

Lehrermaterialien zu diesem Buch finden Sie unter
www.rowohlt.de/downloads/lehrer. Sie können als
kostenloser Download heruntergeladen werden.

8. Auflage März 2011

Originalausgabe
Veröffentlicht im Rowohlt Taschenbuch Verlag,
Reinbek bei Hamburg, April 2006
Copyright © 2006 by Rowohlt Verlag GmbH,
Reinbek bei Hamburg
Lektorat Christiane Steen
Umschlagillustration Barbara Korthues
Umschlaggestaltung any.way, Andreas Pufal
Alle Rechte vorbehalten
Satz Minion PostScript (InDesign)
bei Pinkuin Satz und Datentechnik, Berlin
Druck und Bindung Druckerei C. H. Beck, Nördlingen
Printed in Germany
ISBN 978 3 499 21352 6

Das für dieses Buch verwendete FSC®-zertifizierte Papier
Lux Cream liefert Stora Enso, Finnland.

Inhalt

*Chapter One – **Das fängt ja gut an!***   7

*Kapitel Zwei – **Friend-ly Advice***   10

*Chapter Three – **E-Mail für Britney***   14

*Kapitel Vier – **Getting Ready to Leave***   17

*Chapter Five – **Eine laaaaange Reise***   19

*Kapitel Sechs – **At Chicago Airport***   21

*Chapter Seven – **Wer ist wer?***   23

*Kapitel Acht – **Welcome to Appleton***   27

*Chapter Nine – **Sonntagmorgenkrach***   31

*Kapitel Zehn – **Bad Mood, Good Breakfast***   34

*Chapter Eleven – **Bei Madison***   38

*Kapitel Zwölf – **Roosevelt High School***   41

*Chapter Thirteen – **Viele Informationen***   45

*Kapitel Vierzehn – **Girl Talk***   51

*Chapter Fifteen – **«Coole» Milchshakes***   53

*Kapitel Sechzehn – **The Big City***   58

*Chapter Seventeen – **Wo bitte geht's zu McDonald's?***   66

*Kapitel Achtzehn – **Six Flags, Home of the Penny Trick***   76

*Chapter Nineteen – **Das Fußballturnier***   91

*Kapitel Zwanzig – **Finally Spring Break***   101

Chapter Twenty-one – **Deutsche Wurzeln** *104*

Kapitel Zweiundzwanzig –

That's Some Bad Weather out There! *107*

Chapter Twenty-three – **Immer mit der Ruhe** *110*

Kapitel Vierundzwanzig – **Tornado!** *116*

Chapter Twenty-five – **Endspurt** *123*

Kapitel Sechsundzwanzig – **Goodbye, America** *125*

Epilogue – **Nachwort** *127*

Chapter One –
Das fängt ja gut an!

Tobias rutschte unruhig auf seinem Stuhl herum. Nur noch ein paar Minuten, dann war die sechste Stunde vorbei und *endlich* Wochenende. Wie sich der Unterricht aber auch immer hinzog, besonders Englisch und besonders freitags. Diese Hausaufgaben könnte man doch bestimmt auch schneller vergleichen … Endlich klingelte es zum Stundenende. Tobias steckte hastig sein Buch und den Kugelschreiber in den Rucksack und war schon fast aus der Tür, als er Frau Berger gegen den Lärm rufen hörte: «Die Schülerinnen und Schüler, die Ostern am Austausch teilnehmen, bleiben bitte noch fünf Minuten hier!» «Na, phantastisch», dachte Tobias und ließ sich auf den nächstbesten Stuhl fallen.

Der Austausch war die Idee seiner Mutter gewesen. Wem sonst würde es einfallen, ihn drei Wochen ans andere Ende der Welt zu schicken, nur um seine Noten aufzubessern? Tobias Stein zumindest nicht. Was ihn anging, war eine Vier minus in Englisch keine große Sache, und auf Osterferien ohne seine besten Freunde hatte er auch keine Lust. Wenn es nach New York gehen würde oder an den Strand nach Kalifornien, das wäre etwas anderes, aber wer hatte denn je etwas von Wisconsin gehört?

8000 kilometers away, Britney Summerfield jumped out of the Kimballs' minivan in front of her parents' house. It was only eight o'clock in the evening, but Britney felt like it was midnight. She had had a long day at school: classes until three o'clock, then a break for homework, and finally, soccer practice. «I can't wait for spring break!» Britney thought. She closed the minivan's side-door and waved goodbye to the Kimballs. Madison Kimball was Britney's best friend, and her mom, Mrs Kimball, always picked the girls up from soccer practice. Britney went inside the house.

Mrs Summerfield was in the living room, watching TV. «Hi darling, how was your day?» she said when Britney entered.

«Don't ask,» Britney sighed and plunged down on the sofa. «I'm so tired, I think I'll go straight to bed.»

Her Mom smiled at her. «I saved some dinner for you – chicken and mashed potatoes. You should really eat before you go to sleep.»

«Food does sound like a good idea,» Britney thought. She got up and walked into the kitchen. While she waited for her food to warm up in the microwave she spotted a letter on the kitchen table. Britney was surprised to see that it had her name on it. She hardly ever got mail. She did get e-mail, of course, but never really any real letters. She took a closer look at the envelope and saw that it was from her school. «Oh,» Britney thought, «I think I know what this is.» She opened the letter and began reading.

«Wie bitte?!!» Entsetzt schaute Tobias seine Lehrerin an. «Ist das Ihr Ernst?!» Frau Berger schmunzelte.

«Tobias, dieser Austausch ist eine so große Chance für dich, du solltest dich freuen, dass wir eine Gastfamilie für dich gefunden haben!»

«Aber …», begann Tobias verzweifelt und starrte auf den Zettel in seiner Hand. Er konnte es nicht glauben. «Ich hatte doch extra angekreuzt, dass ich einen Gast*bruder* haben will!»

«Tut mir Leid, Tobias», sagte Frau Berger. «Wir konnten nicht alle Wünsche berücksichtigen. Ich bin sicher, du wirst dich mit deiner Gastschwester bestens verstehen.»

Tobias schüttelte wütend den Kopf, stopfte den Zettel in seine Hosentasche und stürmte aus dem Klassenzimmer.

«Hey Mom,» Britney yelled, «take a look at this!»

«What's going on, darling?» Mrs Summerfield appeared in the kitchen door. Her daughter looked very upset.

«Remember the German exchange student who is coming to stay with us?» Britney said angrily.

«Of course I do, what is the matter?»

«I asked for a girl, but they are sending a boy! Or … do you think Tobias is a girl's name in Germany?»

«No honey, I don't think so.» Mrs Summerfield smiled. «I guess you'll have a brother for three weeks.»

«Great,» Britney sighed. «Just when I thought my day couldn't get any worse.»

Tobias lag auf seinem Bett und starrte an die Decke.

«Drei Wochen in diesem Zimmer wären besser als dieser bescheuerte Austausch», dachte er wütend. Drei Wochen Wisconsin. Keine Ahnung, wo das überhaupt war. Drei Wochen ohne Matthias, Philipp und Jonas, ohne den Inliner-Park und Rollerhockey, ohne Fußballtraining jeden Dienstag.

Zum x-ten Mal las er den Zettel, den Frau Berger ihm gegeben hatte. Drei Wochen in Wisconsin. Mit einem Mädchen. Und was war Britney überhaupt für ein alberner Name? Tobias knüllte den Zettel zusammen und feuerte ihn quer durchs Zimmer, direkt in den Papierkorb.

Kapitel Zwei – *Friend-ly Advice* ✈

There was no school on Saturday morning, but just about everyone that Britney knew from school had come to Plamann Park for the soccer games. All the Fox Valley High Schools had sent their teams, and everybody was very excited. Britney and Madison were walking to the park pavilion to use the drinking fountain.

«Do you think we're going to win today?» Madison asked. «I heard that Appleton East has some great new players.»

«Oh, I don't know.» Britney said. Her mind was not focused on soccer today. There was something else she wanted to discuss with her friend. «Do you remember that exchange program with Germany?»

Madison had been Britney's best friend since the first grade, and she understood at once that something had to be wrong. «Of course, why?» Madison asked.

«They're sending a boy!» Britney said.

«No way!» Madison was very surprised. «That's not even allowed, is it?»

«Yes, it is,» sighed Britney. «And my parents think that it's no problem at all.» Madison took a drink from the water fountain and said: «My parents wouldn't let me host a boy. That's for sure. They are much stricter than yours.» «I didn't think I would ever say this,» Britney replied, «but I really wish my parents were stricter.»

Madison smiled. «You know, maybe he'll be cute. Do you think he'll be wearing Lederhosen and that weird German hat?» Britney didn't think that her friend was funny at all. «I don't care,» she said angrily, taking a big drink of water. They heard Coach Henderson yell for the team to get ready and started jogging back to the field. «Maybe you can still change your parents' minds,» Madison suggested. Britney didn't answer. «I really don't think that I could change my parents' minds,» she thought to herself. «But maybe Madison is right – maybe that German boy will be cute …»

Tobias saß auf einer Bank zwischen zwei Halfpipes und schnürte seine Rollerblades. Jonas, Matthias und Philipp waren schon auf dem betonierten Platz in der Mitte des Inliner-Parks.

«Hey, Tobias», rief Jonas, «beeil dich, wir wollen anfangen!»

«Zwei gegen zwei», rief Matthias, «du und Jonas gegen Philipp und mich.»

Tobias schnappte sich seinen Hockeyschläger und lief zu seinen Freunden. Nachdem sie eine Dreiviertelstunde gespielt hatten und Philipp und Matthias mit 16 zu 12 Toren in Führung lagen, ließ Jonas sich erschöpft am Spielfeldrand fallen. «Time out!», rief er außer Atem.

«Ich könnte auch 'ne Pause gebrauchen», sagte Tobias.

«Also, Tobi, was höre ich da eigentlich für Geschichten über dich?», wollte Jonas wissen, als er wieder zu Atem gekommen war.

«Was meinst du?», fragte Tobias verwundert.

«Genau», grinste Matthias, «wir haben gehört, du hast 'ne neue Freundin in Aussicht!»

«Was?!?» Tobias war jetzt völlig verwirrt.

«Und nicht nur irgendeine Freundin», warf Philipp ein, «sondern eine amerikanische Pop-Prinzessin!»

Matthias verschluckte sich vor Lachen fast an seinem Isodrink.

Langsam dämmerte es Tobias. Der Austausch! Und Britney! «Ihr seid Idioten», murmelte er gereizt. «Hört bloß auf damit!»

«War nicht so gemeint, Kumpel.» Matthias klopfte ihm entschuldigend auf die Schulter. Dann fügte er hinzu: «Hauptsache, du bringst uns Autogramme mit!»

Philipp und Jonas konnten sich vor Lachen kaum halten.

Tobias lächelte gequält. Er wusste, wenn er sich jetzt auf eine langwierige Erklärung einlassen würde, dass es sich bei dieser Britney *natürlich nicht* um die Sängerin Britney Spears handelte, würde er wahrscheinlich nur noch weitere Lachanfälle seiner Freunde riskieren. Also nahm Tobias seinen Hockeyschläger und stand auf. «Zweites Drittel», sagte er nur, «auf geht's.»

Als Tobias am Abend mit seinen Eltern am Esstisch saß, hatte sich seine Laune noch immer nicht gebessert. Gedankenverloren starrte er auf seinen Teller.

«Was ist los, Tobi?», fragte sein Vater.

«Du bist so still heute!», fügte seine Mutter hinzu.

«Dieser blöde Austausch, zu dem du mich überredet hast!», rutschte es ihm heraus. «Ich will nicht nach Wisconsin, und ich will schon gar nicht zu dieser blöden Britney!»

«Warte es doch erst mal ab!», antwortete seine Mutter. «Vielleicht ist diese Britney ja ganz nett!»

Tobias schaute sie kopfschüttelnd an.

«Mama hat Recht», sagte Herr Stein. «Warum e-mailst du ihr nicht und stellst dich vor, vielleicht lernst du sie dann gleich ein bisschen besser kennen!»

«Meine Eltern verstehen mich überhaupt nicht», dachte Tobias bei sich. Andererseits … vielleicht war die Idee mit der E-Mail gar nicht so verkehrt. Verschlechtern konnte sich seine Lage dadurch auch nicht mehr. Er half seinem Vater schnell beim Tischabräumen und lief dann in sein Zimmer. Er fischte den zerknitterten Zettel aus dem Papierkorb und startete seinen Computer.

Chapter Three –
E-Mail für Britney ✈

The Summerfield family had just finished their dinner, and Britney decided that it would be a great time to check her e-mail. «Dad is probably already asleep on the couch,» she thought to herself and smiled, «and Mom will be too lazy to get up, too. I'll have the computer all to myself.»

She started up the computer and went online. She typed in the address of her e-mail provider and, once that page opened, she typed in her e-mail address, and her secret password. Her mailbox opened. Britney liked writing letters to her friends, and she was always a little excited when her new e-mails appeared on the screen. Today, there was only one new e-mail. She didn't recognize the address, but then she looked a little bit closer.

Sender: Tobias Stein.

Tobias. The German boy. Britney sighed. This wasn't exciting; it was just bad news. She clicked on Tobias' name. The e-mail opened and Britney started reading.

```
To: Britney Summerfield
From: Tobias Stein
Subject: Austausch


Hello Britney,
my name is Tobias. I'm from Germany. Do you
speak German? I hope so. Ich komme in deine
Familie. Mit dem Austausch. Und ich wollte
mich vorstellen. Ich versuche es mal wieder
auf Englisch, bin aber nicht so gut.
I'm 15 years old. I'm in the 9th grade. My
hobbies are: football and inline skating.
My parents are teachers. I have no sisters
or brothers. Do you have a brother?
I live in Göttingen. That's almost in the
middle of Germany. How is Wisconsin? Und
was sind deine Hobbys?
Tobias
```

The e-mail was short, but it took Britney quite some time to read it. After all, she had only been learning German for two years. She got out her dictionary and looked up *Austausch* and *vorstellen* and *eigentlich*. Now it all made a lot more sense. «At least this Tobias boy seems to be pretty good at English,» Britney thought. «And he likes sports, that's not bad.» She looked at the e-mail again. «I guess I could just write him back and try to be nice,» Britney decided. She clicked the «reply» button on the screen and started typing.

To: Tobias Stein
From: Britney Summerfield
Subject: RE: Austausch

Hi Tobias,
danke für die Mail. Ich kann nicht sprechen
viel auf Deutsch. Ich lerne Deutsch in der
Schule. Ich bin 15 Jahre alt.
As you can see, my German isn't as good as
your English. I'm in the ninth grade, too.
I like sports, too, especially soccer. I
think soccer and European football are the
same thing. Maybe we can play together when
you come here.
My mom is a nurse and my dad is a dentist.
I have a little sister, her name is Brianne
and she is 5 years old.
Here is some information about Wisconsin.
It's by Lake Michigan, and Milwaukee is the
biggest city around here. Sometimes people
call us cheeseheads, which means Kase-Kopfe
(how do you make those dots over the letters
on a computer keyboard? I can't find them on
mine!). There are many cows here and
Wisconsin macht viel Kase (with the dots
over the <a> again).
Write me if you have any more questions.
Otherwise I will see you in a week.
Bis dann,
Britney

Kapitel Vier –
Getting Ready to Leave ✈

Es war bereits eine knappe Woche vergangen, seit Tobias die Antwort von Britney gelesen hatte. Die Mail war ja ganz okay, aber manches fand er ein bisschen blöd. Eine kleine Schwester half ihm schon mal gar nicht weiter; er hatte insgeheim auf einen Bruder gehofft. Und Wisconsin war berühmt für Kühe und Käse? Das klang ja nicht gerade aufregend. Und diese Britney behauptete tatsächlich, sie würde Fußball spielen? Tobias kannte kein Mädchen, das sich überhaupt für Fußball interessierte.

Und dann wollte sie auch noch *mit ihm* spielen! «Lächerlich!», dachte Tobias. «So weit kommt es noch, dass ich mit einem Mädchen kicke!»

Dann fiel ihm wieder ein, was Jonas und Matthias gesagt hatten. Fußball hin oder her, vielleicht war diese Britney nachher doch ganz süß! Eine amerikanische Freundin hatte zumindest noch keiner seiner Freunde gehabt …

In diesen Gedanken versunken hatte Tobias den großen Koffer aus dem Keller geholt und stand jetzt vor seinem Kleiderschrank. Es war Donnerstag. Übermorgen ging es los, es wurde also langsam Zeit zu packen. Seine Mutter hatte ihm schon ein paar Sachen zurechtgelegt, aber Tobias wollte doch lieber selbst seine Lieblingsklamotten heraussuchen. Jeans, T-Shirts, ein paar Kapuzenpullis … das müsste eigentlich reichen. Oder hatte er etwas vergessen? Er schaute sich seinen Schrank noch einmal genau an und überlegte. Einen Moment zögerte er. Dann warf er seine Fußballschuhe auch in den Koffer.

It was Saturday afternoon and Britney was in the guestroom of the Summerfield's house. This was the bedroom where that German boy would be sleeping in just a couple of hours. «His name is Tobias!» she reminded herself. She had to start using his name instead of calling him «that German boy» all the time.

Mrs Summerfield had told her to fix up the room for him. «His room,» her mom had said, and Britney had felt very strange. His e-mail had sounded really nice, she had to admit, but what if Tobias wasn't nice at all but some ... sauerkraut-eating idiot? She didn't even want to think about it.

No matter what, Britney had to concentrate on fixing «his» bedroom. But what should she do? She had already taken out blue bed sheets. Now ... what else?

Her mom had said: «Make it nice and cozy for Tobias! We want him to feel at home here,» Britney remembered. «Cozy ...» she thought. Should she get a teddy bear from her sister's room and place it on the bed?

‹That's childish,› she decided.

Maybe some flowers from the family room?

«He's not grandma,» Britney thought to herself.

She'd have to think of something else.

«Britney darling, are you ready? It's time to go to the airport and pick up your ‹new brother›!» her father's voice called cheerfully from downstairs.

Britney rolled her eyes. What could she use for decoration? She had to hurry!

«Britney! Come on!» her father shouted again.

«Just a second!» she yelled back. She went into her own room and put on a hooded sweatshirt. On her way out the door she had an idea. She ripped the poster of the national women's soccer team off the wall. She also took some Scotch tape, went back to the guestroom and put the poster up over Tobias's bed.

«Much better!» she thought and dashed down the stairs to meet her father.

Chapter Five –
Eine laaaaange Reise ✈

Tobias gähnte und guckte auf seine Armbanduhr. Noch zwei Stunden bis zur Landung! Er wusste zwar nicht, was ihn in den USA erwarten würde, doch er konnte es kaum abwarten, aus diesem Flugzeug herauszukommen. Anfangs hatte es ihm noch Spaß gemacht, das Meer anzusehen, die Wolken und den Sonnenuntergang zu beobachten. Aber langsam reichte es! Sieben Stunden eingepfercht in diesem Flieger waren wirklich genug! Das Essen hatte ihm auch nicht geschmeckt – lauwarme Spaghetti mit matschigem Salat und zum Nachtisch irgendeine komische Creme.

Tobias guckte sich um. Der Film, der zur Unterhaltung der

Reisenden gezeigt worden war, war längst vorbei, die meisten Leute schliefen oder lasen Zeitung. Um Tobias herum saßen einige Schüler, die wie er am Austausch teilnahmen. Doch auch der Junge neben ihm am Gang schlief: Er schnarchte mit offenem Mund und lehnte sich weit – viel zu weit für Tobias' Geschmack! – in seine Richtung.

Als Gesprächspartnerin blieb also nur das Mädchen neben ihm am Fenster. Er wusste, dass sie in seine Parallelklasse ging und Anna hieß, hatte aber noch nie ein Wort mit ihr gewechselt. Er hatte keine Ahnung, wie er ein Gespräch mit ihr anfangen sollte.

«Ähem», machte Tobias in Richtung des Mädchens.

Sie blickte ihn fragend an und schaute dann wieder aus dem Fenster.

Das hatte schon mal nicht funktioniert! Tobias hustete ein wenig, räusperte sich und sagte noch einmal «ähem», dieses Mal mit einem Lächeln zum Fenster hin.

«Hast du irgendwas gesagt?», fragte Anna.

«Äh, ja. Ich meine, ich wollte fragen, ob du auch den Austausch mitmachst», antwortete Tobias verlegen.

«Blöde Frage. Natürlich mache ich mit. Sonst wäre ich wohl nicht hier!», antwortete Anna genervt. «Ich hatte letztes Jahr in Englisch nur eine Zwei plus, weißt du», schob sie etwas freundlicher nach.

«Oh!», sagte Tobias. Um gar nicht erst auf seine Englischnote zu sprechen zu kommen, versuchte er es lieber mit einem Witz: «Ich fahre mit, weil ich mir mal die ganzen Käseköpfe und ihre Kühe angucken will!»

Anna sah ihn verwirrt an. «Du glaubst doch nicht, dass das alles ist, oder? Ich meine, es ist doch klar, dass es in Wisconsin auch richtig beeindruckende Städte gibt. Also, ich habe gelesen» – sie tippte auf ein dickes Buch in der Sitztasche vor ihr, das Tobias erst jetzt bemerkte – «dass Milwaukee und Madison total groß sind. Und unsere Stadt, Appleton, hat auch 80 000 Einwohner. Ich glaube kaum, dass es da viele Kühe gibt!» Mit diesen Worten drehte Anna sich demonstrativ zum Fenster zurück.

«Was für eine Zicke!», dachte Tobias ärgerlich. Er schickte ein Stoßgebet zum Himmel, dass Britney wenigstens ein bisschen cooler sein würde als diese Streberin neben ihm.

Kapitel Sechs –
At Chicago Airport ✈

Britney and Mr Summerfield had driven all the way to Chicago in their Buick. It had taken them three and a half hours to get to O'Hare Airport. When they entered the international terminal Britney spotted Madison and her dad. They were talking to Mrs Mayers, the German teacher. Almost all of the students from Britney's German class stood around them. Everybody seemed very happy and excited. Britney and Mr Summerfield walked over to the group.

«Hey Brit!» Madison gave her best friend a big smile. «Are you excited about meeting your German boy?»

Britney smiled back at her, and, not for the first time today, she had a funny feeling in her stomach. She really *was* excited!

«I guess I am,» Britney admitted. «How about you?»

Madison answered: «I can't wait to meet your guy … Tobias. That's his name, right? My partner's name is Anna, by the way.»

Britney sighed. «Are you sure you don't want to swap, you take Tobias and I take Anna?»

Madison laughed. «I'd like to, but …»

She stopped talking mid-sentence and pointed to the glass door in front of her. On the other side was a huge group of students, all carrying big bags and pulling suitcases. They all looked very tired.

«Too late for discussions, Britney,» Madison said. «Here come the Germans!»

Dieses blöde Gepäck! Tobias zog mühsam seinen Überseekoffer hinter sich her. Gleichzeitig versuchte er, seinen Pass aus dem Rucksack zu fischen. Gar nicht so einfach, dabei mit den anderen Schülern Schritt zu halten. Endlich hatte er es geschafft und konnte sich in der Schlange für die Passkontrolle anstellen. Tobias gähnte. «Hoffentlich geht das hier schnell», dachte er. Nach neun Stunden Flug hatte er wirklich keine Lust mehr, sich lange anzustellen. Endlich ging es voran, und die Schülerinnen und Schüler bewegten sich schrittweise durch die Passkontrolle. Jetzt war Tobias an der Reihe. Die Beamtin warf einen Blick auf seine Unterlagen und wünschte ihm dann mit strengem Blick einen «nice stay in the United States».

«Den wünsche ich mir auch», murmelte Tobias.

Er nahm seinen Koffer und trottete zu seinen Mitschülern, die sich auf der anderen Seite der Passkontrolle um Frau Berger sammelten. Ein paar Meter von ihnen entfernt war eine große Glastür mit einem grünen EXIT-Schild. Tobias' Blick fiel auf die große Gruppe Wartender auf der anderen Seite. Ob das ihre Austauschpartner waren, die dort auf «die Deutschen» warteten? Plötzlich wurde ihm bewusst, dass Britney auch dort draußen stehen würde. Er suchte die Menge nach einem Mädchen ab, das so aussah, als hieße es Britney. Dabei fiel ihm auf, dass er – Matthias und Jonas sei Dank! – immer noch das Bild der blonden Popsängerin vor Augen hatte. Er wusste gar nicht, wie diese Britney wirklich aussah! Er ließ seinen Blick noch einmal über die Gruppe schweifen, doch es waren einfach zu viele Menschen hinter der Tür. Die Stimme seiner Englischlehrerin riss Tobias aus seinen Gedanken. «Ich glaube, wir sind vollzählig! Los geht's!»

Chapter Seven –
Wer ist wer? ✈

Britney and Madison had fallen silent. Like the rest of their classmates they were staring at the big glass door that had just opened. When the first tired-looking boys and girls emerged, everyone took a deep breath. So these were the Germans! This *was* exciting!

Mrs Mayers rushed forward and started talking to a woman who had to be the Germans' teacher. The two teachers took out long lists and started to match the German students and their American families.

«Madison! Where's Madison Kimball?» Mrs Mayers yelled and looked around.

Britney looked at her friend and noticed that her friend's face had turned pink. Madison looked back at Britney, smiled a weak smile and walked off towards the teachers to meet her partner.

Now Britney was alone with her father. «Let's go up to Mrs Mayers, and find that Tobias boy,» he suggested. «Okay,» she mumbled shakily and moved towards the teachers. As they got closer they could hear the chatting, laughing and discussion in both English and German. Then she heard someone call her name.

«Britney Summerfield?» asked an unfamiliar voice with an unfamiliar accent. It was the teacher from Germany. Britney nodded. She was too excited to speak. «And you must be Mr Summerfield. I'm Mrs Berger.» The woman shook Mr Summerfield's hand. Then she smiled at Britney. «And your German student should be … let me see,» she checked her list, «oh yes. Tobias Stein.» She turned around and called out something in German. Britney didn't understand a word, but she was sure she had heard Tobias' name.

«Tobias, kommst du bitte her?» Tobias zuckte zusammen, als er seinen Namen hörte. Jetzt wurde es ernst. Er atmete tief durch, packte den Griff seines Koffers und setzte sich in Bewegung. Neben Frau Berger stand noch eine Frau, das musste Mrs Mayers sein. Auf der anderen Seite war ein großer Mann mit einer Baseballmütze, der ihn freundlich ansah. Und neben diesem Mann stand ein Mädchen. Sie war ungefähr so groß wie er selbst, hatte kinnlanges, braunes Haar und trug ziemlich sportliche Klamotten: Turnschuhe, ausgefranste Jeans und einen leuchtend roten Kapuzenpulli. Im Moment hüpfte sie von einem Bein aufs andere und lächelte etwas verlegen in seine Richtung.

«Tobias, das sind Britney und ihr Vater», stellte Frau Berger die beiden vor.

«Ähh … hello», hörte Tobias sich sagen.

Britney war einen Schritt auf ihn zugetreten und streckte ihm ihre rechte Hand entgegen. «Guten Tag. Ich heiße Britney. Wie geht es Ihnen?», sagte sie etwas mechanisch.

Tobias schaute das Mädchen erstaunt an, schüttelte dann zögernd ihre Hand.

«Ääh … ganz gut», brachte er heraus.

Warum gab dieses Mädchen ihm so spießig die Hand? Und hatte sie gerade wirklich «Sie» zu ihm gesagt?

«Hello Tobias,» Mr Summerfield joined in. «It's great to meet you. Let's get your things into the car and drive home.»

Mit diesen Worten schnappte er sich Tobias' Koffer, winkte Frau Berger und Mrs Mayers noch über die Schulter zu und ging los in Richtung Ausgang. Tobias schaute wieder zu Britney.

«Alright ... let's go,» she said.

«Ääh ... o.k.», antwortete Tobias und stapfte hinter Mr Summerfield und seiner Tochter her.

Mr Summerfield stellte Tobias eine Frage nach der anderen. «How was your flight?»

«Have you been to America before?»

«Do you like American cars?» Und so weiter. Tobias versuchte, all seine Fragen zu beantworten, aber es war richtig schwierig, plötzlich so viel Englisch zu sprechen. Er dachte auch darüber nach, was er zu Britney sagen könnte, aber ihm fiel nicht das Geringste ein.

Sie waren bestimmt schon zehn Minuten auf einem riesigen Parkplatz herumgelaufen, als sie endlich beim Auto der Summerfields ankamen.

«Wow! Das Auto ist ja riesig! Da passt der Golf von Mama dreimal rein!», dachte Tobias. Laut sagte er: «That's a very big car!» Britney und ihr Vater schauten sich an und grinsten.

«This is the *small* car, Tobias», sagte Mr Summerfield, «wait until you see the *other* one!»

Tobias war beeindruckt.

Nachdem Mr Summerfield sein Gepäck im Kofferraum verstaut hatte, setzte Tobias sich auf die Rückbank des Autos. Britney setzte sich auf den Platz neben ihrem Vater. Als Mr Summerfield losfuhr, schaute Tobias sich zum ersten Mal richtig um.

«Das ist also Amerika», dachte er und lehnte sich zurück.

Unmengen von Autos, vierspurige Straßen und hohe Gebäude. Andererseits war das hier noch der Flughafen in Chicago … wie es wohl in Appleton aussah?

Britney had been quiet for a long time. So this was ‹the German boy›. He really was in their car; he really was going to be with them for the next three weeks. «He seems nice,» she thought, «but I wish I knew what to say to him …» Britney tried hard to think of something in German. «Oh, I know something!» But when she turned around she saw that she wouldn't have to say anything for a while:

Tobias had fallen asleep in the back seat.

Kapitel Acht –
Welcome to Appleton ✈

Tobias wachte erst wieder auf, als seine Autotür vorsichtig geöffnet wurde. «Tobias!», flüsterte jemand. Eigentlich klang es mehr wie «To-bei-äs». Tobias schlug verwirrt die Augen auf. Als er das dunkelhaarige Mädchen vor ihm sah, fiel ihm gleich alles wieder ein. Er war in Amerika!

«I'm sorry I woke you up, but we're home!», sagte Britney mit leiser Stimme. Tobias nickte schlaftrunken. Britney lächelte und hielt die Autotür für ihn auf.

«Thank you», murmelte er. Und um ein bisschen mehr zu sagen, fragte er: «How long did I sleep?»

«Almost three hours», antwortete Britney. «Are you hungry now?»

«Ja, total!», rutschte es ihm heraus. «Ich meine, yes. I am hungry.» Britney lächelte und machte eine Handbewegung, ihr zu folgen.

«My mom is in the kitchen, she just made dinner», erklärte sie. «We can eat and …», sie zögerte und fuhr dann mit einem breiten Grinsen fort: «We can eat and … Sie können meine Mom kennen lernen.»

«Good idea», sagte Tobias. Jetzt war er es, der lächelte. Dieses Mädchen hatte ihn tatsächlich schon wieder gesiezt!

Walking up the driveway with Tobias, Britney noticed that he was looking around curiously. Appleton certainly didn't look like the skyscrapers of Chicago, but it looked nice, she found. The houses were all far apart, with big front yards, big side yards, and no fences to separate any of them. They looked very different from one another. Each one looked like someone had had a completely new idea for how a house should be built.

Britney was about to point out the different styles of architecture when she saw that Tobias had spotted something new: He had stopped walking and was looking up at the telephone wires. Three squirrels were climbing around on them.

«This way, Tobias!» said Britney as she walked to the front door of the house. Tobias didn't follow.

«Sorry. I only looked at the …» He pointed to the little animals.

«Oh, the squirrels!» said Britney. «Those are *everywhere*!»

She walked to the door and held it open for Tobias.

«Should I get my suitcase?» Tobias asked as he walked across the big front yard toward Britney. «No, it's cool. My dad will get it.»

The German boy gave her a surprised look.

«Why is that *cool*?» he asked.

«Oh,» Britney smiled. «That just means ‹it's fine› or ‹it's o.k.›»

«Oh, o.k.!» Tobias said. «I didn't know that.»

«We say it all the time,» Britney explained. «You should remember it.»

Tobias nodded and followed her into the house.

«Who's hungry?!!», hörte Tobias eine Stimme rufen, als sie das Haus betraten. Er schaute sich um. Links führte eine Treppe nach oben, und am Ende des Flures vor ihnen lag eine große Küche. Von dort war die Stimme gekommen. Rechts gab es noch ein Wohnzimmer, in das Tobias einen Blick warf, während er Britney in die Küche folgte. Die Möbel im Wohnzimmer sahen ganz schön dunkel und altmodisch aus, fand Tobias. Die Küche dagegen war hell und modern.

«Hi, Tobias, it's nice to meet you!», rief Britneys Mutter, als er ins Zimmer trat. «How are you?»

«Fine, thank you», murmelte Tobias.

«Sorry we don't have anything big planned for dinner», fuhr Mrs Summerfield fort. Sie öffnete die Kühlschranktür und blickte suchend hinein. Britney ging zu der Essbar in der Mitte der Küche und setzte sich auf einen der vier Hochstühle.

«Have a seat, Tobias», sagte sie.

Er wollte gerade auf den Stuhl neben Britney klettern, als sich Mrs Summerfield, deren Kopf noch immer im Küchenschrank steckte, wieder zu Wort meldete.

«O.k., we got mac and cheese, all kinds of soup, chips, nachos, cereal, what do you guys feel like?»

«Ääh, how do I feel?», fragte Tobias, der nur wenig von dieser Flut fremder Wörter verstanden hatte.

«She means, what do you want to eat?», erklärte Britney.

«Oh, I don't know …» Tobias fühlte sich etwas dumm – da wurde er nur gefragt, was er essen wollte, und er hatte keine Ahnung, um was es ging.

«Shall I just fix you something?», fragte Mrs Summerfield lächelnd. «You like pasta, don't you? How about some macaroni?»

Makkaroni! Endlich mal ein Wort, das er kannte. «Yes. Thank you», sagte er erleichtert.

Nachdem er zwei große Teller Makkaroni mit Käsesoße gegessen hatte, fühlte Tobias sich noch müder als zuvor. Er wünschte Britney und ihren Eltern eine gute Nacht und zog sich ins Gästezimmer zurück. Er war zu erschöpft, seinen Koffer auszupacken oder sich das Zimmer genauer anzuschauen. Er zog die schweren Vorhänge zu, krabbelte unter die Bettdecke und schlief sofort ein.

Chapter Nine –
Sonntagmorgenkrach ✈

Britney woke up in the middle of the night. She sat up and looked around in her dark room. What had happened? Everything was quiet. Then she remembered the dream she had just had. She had dreamt that she was at the airport with her father and that they had picked up the German boy, just like they had in reality. In her dream, she had tried to talk to Tobias, but she had suddenly forgotten how to speak German – and English! She remembered that Tobias and her father had laughed at her, and then everybody else at the airport had laughed and pointed their fingers at her. Now Britney knew that she had woken up from that laughter. «What a nightmare!» she thought. Then she smiled to herself. «Thank God I *do* speak English, and some German!» She lay down again and pulled up her blanket. Within a few minutes, she was quietly asleep again.

Als Tobias aufwachte, war es stockfinster. Er versuchte sich zu orientieren, doch es drang kein Lichtstrahl durch den Vorhang. Vorsichtig stieg er aus dem Bett und tastete sich in Richtung Fenster. Dort angekommen, schob er den Vorhang zur Seite. Zu seiner Überraschung war es auch draußen keineswegs helllichter Tag, sondern ebenso düster wie in seinem Zimmer. Tobias tastete sich zurück ins Bett und suchte seine Uhr auf dem Nachttisch. Er hatte sie gestern noch nicht umgestellt, und das digitale Zifferblatt zeigte 12:02. Kurz nach zwölf in Deutschland, minus sieben Stunden … es war erst fünf Uhr morgens!

Und er fühlte sich putzmunter und ausgeschlafen! Diese Zeit-verschiebung hatte ihn völlig durcheinander gebracht.

Tobias versuchte, wieder einzuschlafen, drehte sich von einer Seite zur anderen – doch ihm wurde immer langweiliger. Er nahm seine Uhr und stellte sie im Dunkeln um. Jetzt zeigte sie 05:15. Nach einer Zeit, die ihm wie eine Ewigkeit vorkam, schaute er wieder. Die Uhr zeigte 05:32. Er drehte sich auf die andere Seite, machte die Augen zu, doch es half nichts. 05:37. Er war hellwach.

Tobias stieg wieder aus dem Bett und tastete sich zur Tür. Dort drückte er auf den Lichtschalter. Zum ersten Mal sah er sein Zimmer richtig vor sich. Das Bettzeug und der Vorhang waren dunkelblau, das Bett selbst war riesig und sah ziemlich altmodisch aus. Dann gab es noch einen kleinen Tisch und einen Schrank aus Eichenholz. Über dem Bett hing – Tobias stutzte – ein Poster, das eine Fußballmannschaft zeigte. Interessiert ging er näher heran. Bevor er die Spieler genauer in Augenschein nehmen konnte, entdeckte er einen Schriftzug unterhalb des Bildes. *USA women's soccer* stand da. «Ach, das ist ja nur Frauenfußball», dachte Tobias enttäuscht. «Langweilig.»

Er öffnete seinen Koffer, kramte seine Kulturtasche und ein paar Klamotten hervor und schlich sich ins Badezimmer. Fünf Uhr morgens oder nicht, der Tag konnte beginnen!

Britney got up at eight o'clock. She took a shower and went to the kitchen.

Mrs and Mr Summerfield were already eating breakfast. «Good morning, honey,» Mrs Summerfield said. And before

Britney could say anything she added: «Why don't you go and wake up Tobias? I prepared a big breakfast for the two of you!» Britney nodded, turned around and walked up the stairs again. She went to Tobias's room and knocked. She was afraid that she would be waking him up – again! –, but to her surprise the door swung open right away. There he was, fully dressed and ready to go.

«Good morning!» Tobias shouted happily.

«Hey,» Britney said. «Did you sleep well?»

«Yes,» Tobias said. «But … I woke up … three hours ago!»

«Oh,» Britney replied. «Your body thinks that you are still in Germany. That's called a jet lag, I think.»

«Yes,» Tobias said. Curiously, he couldn't think of anything else to say.

«Uhmm …» Britney also didn't know what to talk about any more. «Uhmm … do you like your room?»

«Yes,» the German boy repeated. He was silent for a moment, then he looked like he had an idea. He grinned at Britney. «I like my room. But I don't like the poster,» he said, and pointed to the picture of the women's national soccer team.

Britney gave him a confused look. «Why not?» she asked.

«I think … that only boys should play soccer,» Tobias said and laughed. «I think soccer is not for girls.»

«What?!» Britney couldn't believe her ears. Here she was, trying to be nice, and this guy was acting like a complete idiot!

She noticed that Tobias had stopped laughing. He looked a little embarrassed. He tried to say something, but Britney had had enough.

«Breakfast is waiting in the kitchen,» she said sharply. «Don't wait for me.»

She turned around, walked over to her room and slammed the door shut.

Kapitel Zehn –
Bad Mood, Good Breakfast ✈

Tobias stand noch etwas verdutzt im Türrahmen und guckte in die Richtung, in die Britney verschwunden war. «Da gebe ich mir Mühe, die Situation etwas aufzulockern, und dann ist die gleich eingeschnappt!», dachte er ärgerlich. «Warum stellt die sich denn so an?» Er zuckte mit den Schultern und machte sich alleine auf den Weg in die Küche. Dort saßen Mrs und Mr Summerfield noch am Tisch. Als Tobias vorsichtig um die Ecke lugte, sprang Mr Summerfield gleich auf und überhäufte ihn mit einem Wortschwall.

«Good morning, how are you?» Ohne eine Antwort abzuwarten, fuhr er fort: «Breakfast is ready. We have bacon and eggs, pancakes, French toast, some fried potatoes … Would you like some syrup on your pancakes … or some sausages … or how about some banana bread?»

Mrs Summerfield fragte: «And what would you like to drink? O. J., fruit punch, cranberry juice … maybe some milk?»

Tobias traute seinen Ohren kaum. Das sollte er alles essen? Zum Frühstück?

«Ääh …», begann er. «I don't know … what is O. J.?»

Mrs Summerfield lächelte ihn an. «Sorry, that's orange juice. I have to remember to slow down. Have you ever had a full American breakfast?»

«No», sagte Tobias. «But I would like to drink some milk.»

«Great», antwortete Mrs Summerfield. «Why don't you get some milk from the fridge, and I'll get you some food. Do you want pancakes?»

Erleichtert nickte Tobias. «Pancakes» klang nach Pfannkuchen, und den Rest hatte er auch verstanden. Er nahm sich ein Glas aus dem Regal und ging zum Kühlschrank, einem riesigen Ungetüm, das von oben bis unten mit Fotos voll gehängt war. Er fand die Milch, schenkte sich ein und setzte sich wie am Abend vorher an die Essbar.

Mr Summerfield fragte: «Do you know where Britney is?»

«In her room, I think», antwortete Tobias.

«Oh, o. k.» Mr Summerfield nickte. «Did you two already make plans for today?»

«No …», sagte Tobias zögerlich. Wie sollte er Mr und Mrs Summerfield bloß erklären, dass Britney sauer auf ihn war?

«You should go to the Kimball's house and meet Madison. She is Britney's best friend, and she's hosting a student, too», schlug Mrs Summerfield vor, die neben ihn getreten war und sein Frühstück vor ihm abstellte. Auf dem Teller türmten sich Pfannkuchen, sicherlich sechs oder sieben, die regelrecht in einem dunkelbraunen Sirup schwammen. Da Mrs und Mr Summerfield schon mit dem Frühstück fertig zu sein schienen, waren die wohl alle für ihn. Tobias nahm sich eine Gabel und begann zu essen. Der Sirup machte die Pfannkuchen ganz schön süß, aber Tobias schmeckten sie ausgezeichnet. «An das Essen hier könnte ich mich gewöhnen», dachte er. Zu Mrs Summerfield sagte er: «The pancakes taste very good, thank you.»

Mrs Summerfield lächelte. «I'm glad you like them. Would you like some more?»

«No, thank you.» Tobias schüttelte den Kopf.

In diesem Moment hörte er Schritte auf der Treppe, und einen Augenblick später kam Britney in die Küche. Ohne Tobias eines Blickes zu würdigen, griff sie sich ein paar Scheiben Toast, nahm die Milch vom Tisch und verschwand ins Wohnzimmer. Mrs und Mr Summerfield guckten erst sich und dann Tobias verwundert an. Dieser zuckte nur hilflos mit den Schultern.

«Why don't I go and talk to Britney», sagte Mrs Summerfield zu ihrem Mann. «And you and Tobias get ready to drive to the Kimball's house.» Mr Summerfield nickte, und Mrs Summerfield folgte Britney ins Wohnzimmer.

Mr Summerfield wandte sich jetzt an Tobias. «Would you like to look at our cars after you finish breakfast?»

«Yes.» Tobias nickte begeistert. «That would be great!»

«O.k. then, I'll take you into the garage in a few minutes!», sagte Mr Summerfield und ließ Tobias allein in der Küche zurück. Aus dem anderen Zimmer konnte er Britneys Stimme hören. Sie klang ziemlich wütend. Tobias wusste nicht, wie er das finden sollte. Er aß langsam seine Pfannkuchen zu Ende, nahm einen großen Schluck Milch und folgte Mr Summerfield in die Garage.

«I don't know how American cars compare to your BMWs and Mercedes, but they work fine for us», sagte Mr Summerfield, als er das Licht in der Garage anknipste. «I guess you saw the Buick already.»

«Yes. It's very nice», antwortete Tobias.

«Ha!», lachte Mr Summerfield. «The Buick? It's really just our A-to-B car.»

«A-to-B?» Über diesen Ausdruck musste Tobias erst mal nachdenken. «Oh yes, I understand. You use it to get from A to B.»

«Right, but it's not our nice car.» Mr Summerfield nickte.

Tobias sah sich den ‹Von A-nach-B›-Buick an. Das Auto war riesiger als das größte deutsche Auto, das er je gesehen hatte. «Wenn das nur das Alltagsauto ist …», dachte er bei sich.

Mr Summerfield deutete auf das Fahrzeug, das hinter dem Buick geparkt war. «And here's the Ford Excursion», sagte er. «I hear they don't have too many of these in Germany, do they?»

Zuerst dachte Tobias, Mr Summerfield hätte einen Kleinlaster in seiner Garage: Das Auto war riesig! Außerdem war es so dreckig, dass man kaum seine Farbe erkennen konnte.

«We just took this one to our cottage on the lake, and it needs a wash. That's why we didn't take it down to Chicago», erklärte Mr Summerfield.

«Sind Sie mit dem Riesending eine Rallye gefahren?», hätte Tobias am liebsten gefragt. Er hatte noch nie ein so verdrecktes Auto gesehen. Um nicht schon wieder mit einem Witz anzuecken, sagte er nur: «Your cars are much bigger than the cars we have.»

«Really? What do your parents drive?», fragte Britneys Vater interessiert.

«We have two Golfs», antwortete Tobias.

«Oh, the little VWs?», sagte Mr Summerfield. «VW» sprach er «vee-double-you» aus.

Tobias wollte gerade antworten, dass einer der «kleinen Golfs» immerhin ein Kombi war, da betrat Britney die Garage. Ohne Tobias eines Blickes zu würdigen, öffnete sie die Beifahrertür des Buicks.

«Let's go, Dad», sagte sie.

Chapter Eleven –
Bei Madison ✈

Britney couldn't wait to see her best friend. And she couldn't wait for Madison to see what an idiot this Tobias boy was. Telling her that girls shouldn't play soccer! What on earth was he thinking?

When the Summerfields' car turned onto the Kimballs' driveway, Britney could see Madison peeping through the living room window. She knew her friend was dying to see «the German boy». «She won't like him any more than I do,» Britney thought as she got out of the car.

Tobias kletterte wie Britney aus dem Auto. Jetzt würde er also Britneys beste Freundin kennen lernen. Wenn das auch so eine

Zicke war, hatte er jetzt schon genug! Und wer würde überhaupt Madisons Austauschpartner sein? Er konnte sich nicht genau erinnern, wer wem zugeteilt worden war.

Bevor er weiter nachdenken konnte, wurde die Eingangstür des Hauses aufgerissen, und ein Mädchen sprang die beiden Stufen herunter auf die Einfahrt.

«Hey guys! Why don't you come in?», rief sie aufgeregt. Wenigstens schien dieses Mädchen nett und freundlich zu sein.

Madison led Britney and Tobias into the living room, where her German partner, Anna, was sitting on the couch. They had been talking about their free time activities, but Madison found her a bit boring: Anna didn't play any sports, she didn't like MTV, she just seemed to be interested in school, and in books Madison had never heard of before.

«O nein!», war Tobias einziger Gedanke, als er Anna auf dem Sofa sitzen sah. Jetzt hatte er nicht nur diese überempfindliche Britney am Hals, sondern auch noch die Streberleiche aus dem Flugzeug!

Britney und Tobias setzten sich auf die Couch. Ein paar Sekunden lang herrschte Stille, dann brach Madison das Schweigen.

«My name is Madison», sagte sie.

Tobias wunderte sich: Das sollte ein Mädchenname sein? Anna hatte offensichtlich seine Gedanken gelesen, denn sie lehnte sich zu ihm herüber und sagte: «Madison. So wie die

Stadt. In den USA gibt es oft Namen in dieser Art.» Tobias nickte genervt. Dann ergriff Madison selbst wieder das Wort.

«You are Tobias, aren't you? Did I say your name right?», fragte sie.

Madison sprach seinen Namen genauso aus wie Britney. Das hieß, bevor sie aufgehört hatte, mit ihm zu reden. «To-bei-äs».

«Yes, almost. In German my name is pronounced To-bi-as», antwortete er mit einem Seitenblick auf Britney.

«Oh, okay», nickte Madison. Sie wiederholte seinen Namen ein paarmal, aber Tobias fand, es klang immer noch mehr wie ‹To-bei-äs›. Dann sagte Madison: «Ihr Name ist sehr schwierig.»

Tobias grinste. Ständig wurde er hier gesiezt!

«*Dein* Name!», sagte er.

Madison guckte ihn verwundert an. «Why my name?», fragte sie.

«No, no», Tobias lachte. «You can say: *Dein* Name ist schwierig. *Ihr* is only for adults!» Madison und Britney schienen beide überrascht zu sein.

«But Mrs Mayers said …», begann Madison. Doch bevor sie ihren Satz beenden konnte, mischte Anna sich wieder in das Geschehen ein. «Ich habe mich informiert, Tobias», begann sie hochtrabend, «dass Schüler in den USA oft die höfliche Anredeform beigebracht bekommen. Das ist kein Grund, sich lustig zu machen.»

«Ich mache mich gar nicht lustig!», protestierte Tobias. Warum wollte ihn hier eigentlich jeder falsch verstehen?

Anna rümpfte nur die Nase und wandte sich von ihm ab.

«What are we going to do this week?», fragte sie die beiden Amerikanerinnen in perfektem Englisch.

«Well, from tomorrow until Friday, you two can come to school with us. That should be fun! And in the afternoons we have soccer practice. Would you like to come to that, too?», fragte Madison.

Britney warf Tobias einen unfreundlichen Blick zu und sagte in sarkastischem Ton: «I'm sure Tobias would *love* to come to soccer practice!»

Kapitel Zwölf –
Roosevelt High School ✈

Am nächsten Morgen wurde Tobias durch das Knarren des Fußbodens vor seiner Tür geweckt. Wahrscheinlich war es wie am Tag zuvor noch viel zu früh, um aufzustehen. Ihm fiel nichts ein, was er tun könnte, außer im Bett zu liegen und zu warten, bis ihn jemand zum Frühstück rief. Er konnte versuchen, wieder einzuschlafen, oder er konnte sich natürlich das blöde Poster über seinem Bett angucken ...

Wieder hörte er die alten Holzdielen im Flur knarren. Dann schlug eine Tür zu. Offensichtlich war auch schon jemand anderes wach. Nach einiger Zeit hörte er noch mehr Schritte, Türen wurden geöffnet und geschlossen, er hörte leise Stimmen. Dann hörte er eine lautere Stimme direkt vor seinem Zimmer.

«Oh my god, I almost forgot to wake up Tobias!», rief Mrs Summerfield und klopfte energisch an seine Tür.

«Ja …?!», sagte Tobias. Die Tür öffnete sich einen Spalt, und Mrs Summerfield lugte in sein Zimmer.

«Good morning, Tobias. Did you sleep well?», fragte sie. Doch bevor er antworten konnte, fuhr sie fort: «There's breakfast downstairs: Cereal or bagels. If you want to take a shower, you'll have to hurry just a little bit. O.k.?»

«Ääh, yes, o.k.», antwortete er etwas überrumpelt von diesen ganzen Informationen.

Ten minutes later, Tobias walked down the stairs, his hair still a little bit wet from his quick shower, and found his way to the kitchen. Britney's mom was already there. «I made you a bagel with cream cheese that you can eat in the car. We really have to get going, I'm sorry I didn't wake you up earlier.»

«Okay …» was all Tobias could think to say. He heard someone enter the kitchen behind him and turned around. It was Britney.

«Guten Morgen, Tobias,» she said in the sweetest voice and with a big smile. Then she stopped smiling and turned to her mom. «There you go, mom, was that okay?»

Mrs Summerfield did not like her daughter's behavior. «Britney!» she said angrily. But Britney only shrugged her shoulders.

Mrs Summerfield sighed and turned to Tobias. «Are you ready to go, or do you need anything else, something to drink?»

«Is there any tea?» Tobias asked.

«Tea??!!» Britney sounded as if he had asked for a glass of green slime.

«No time for tea, Tobias, sorry,» said Mrs Summerfield, ignoring her daughter's behavior. «Here's a bottle of juice you can drink in the car. We better get going.»

«Come on!» said Britney impatiently and left the kitchen for the garage.

Im Buick schaute Tobias aus dem Fenster und sah Appleton an sich vorbeiziehen, während er seinen Bagel mit Creamcheese aß. Er saß auf der Rückbank, während Britney mit ihrer Mutter vorne saß. Offenbar stritten sie wegen irgendetwas, aber Tobias konnte sie über das Radio hinweg nicht verstehen.

Schließlich hielten sie an einem großen Klinkergebäude mit einer riesigen Rasenfläche davor. Ein großes Schild verkündete «Roosevelt High School».

Britney warf einen Blick auf die Uhr. «Oh great, we're going to be late», stöhnte sie.

Tobias griff nach seinem Rucksack und der Saftflasche.

«Leave the bottle here, Tobias. You can't bring drinks into the school», sagte Mrs Summerfield. Tobias wollte schon fragen, warum man das nicht durfte, aber offenbar war keine Zeit mehr dafür.

«Come on, let's go. I don't want a detention», sagte Britney ungeduldig, als Tobias die Flasche an Mrs Summerfield zurückgab. Ohne zu warten, ging sie in Richtung Schule davon.

«I'm coming.» Tobias lief ihr nach, und sie eilten durch die Eingangstüren des Schulgebäudes.

«What is detention?», fragte Tobias vorsichtig.

Britney verdrehte die Augen. Dann sagte sie: «You get detention when you're late. Or when you do something else that is against school rules.»

«Vielleicht ist das so was Ähnliches wie Nachsitzen», dachte Tobias bei sich.

Gerade als sie den Klassenraum erreichten, ertönte die Schulglocke.

Die anderen Schülerinnen und Schüler saßen schon auf ihren Plätzen, als Britney mit Tobias im Schlepptau durch die Tür trat.

«Have a seat, Ms Summerfield, you *just* made it,» the teacher said. He was sitting at his desk, in front of a computer. The nametag on the desk said, «Mr MASON.»

Mr Mason gave Tobias a surprised look. «So, who's your friend, Britney?»

«The German exchange student?» Britney answered, but sounded like she was asking a question. «His name is … Toe-by-as.»

«Das hat sie doch jetzt mit Absicht schön falsch ausgesprochen», dachte Tobias ärgerlich.

«Oh, that's right. Well, get him a chair. Welcome to Roosevelt High School, Tobias,» said Mr Mason.

Without another word, Britney took a plastic chair from the back of the room and set it next to her desk. Tobias sat down.

He could feel thirty sets of eyes staring at him, and there were some giggles from somewhere in the room.

Chapter Thirteen –
Viele Informationen ✈

Endlich Mittagspause! Tobias ging mit dem Strom der anderen Schüler in Richtung Cafeteria. Der Vormittag hatte sich lange hingezogen: Erst Geschichte bei Mr Mason, dann Mathe bei einer Lehrerin, deren Namen er vergessen hatte. Der Stoff schien gar nicht so schwer, aber ständig so viel Englisch zu hören, war immer noch anstrengend. Nach Mathe war dann eine Doppelstunde Deutsch an der Reihe gewesen. Tobias hatte sich gefreut, endlich seine Mitschüler aus Deutschland wiederzusehen, aber wie es der Zufall so wollte, hatte er dann doch wieder zwischen Britney, Anna und Madison gesessen. Diese drei waren es jetzt auch, die neben ihm her zur Schulcafeteria gingen. Madison und Britney hatten sich untergehakt und schienen bester Laune. Anna hielt einen Stift und einen karierten Schreibblock in der Hand und machte sich Notizen zu allem, was um sie herum geschah.

«How many students go to this school?», fragte sie die beiden Amerikanerinnen.

«About two thousand, I think», antwortete Madison.

«So viele?», dachte Tobias. «Kein Wunder, dass die anderen aus Deutschland schon wieder wie vom Erdboden verschluckt sind!»

Anna schien auch ein wenig überrascht, eifrig schrieb sie diese neue Information auf. «How many years do you go to high school?», fragte sie dann.

Diesmal antwortete Britney. «Four years. From ninth to twelfth grade.» Auch das schrieb Anna auf.

«When is school out in the afternoon?»

«Classes are done at three-thirty», sagte Britney.

«But after that, we always go to soccer practice», fügte Madison hinzu. «So we normally get home from school at around five or six.»

Anna nickte und notierte sich auch diese Information.

«Schreibst du dir *alles* auf, was hier so passiert?», fragte Tobias ungläubig.

«Natürlich», antwortete Anna und schaute kurz von ihrem Block auf. «Nur so kann man einen Überblick über alle neuen Informationen behalten.»

Sie blätterte in ihrem Block. «Wusstest du zum Beispiel, dass hier nicht die Klassen ihre festen Klassenräume haben, sondern die Lehrer? Und dass die Schüler von einem Fachraum zum nächsten gehen, anstatt dass die Lehrer zu ihnen kommen?» Das war Tobias tatsächlich schon aufgefallen. Er nickte. Anna kam jetzt richtig in Fahrt. «Und hast du gesehen, dass alle Schüler hier einen eigenen Schrank haben? Und dass die Schule einen riesigen Sportplatz hat? *Jeder* nimmt hier nachmittags an Arbeitsgemeinschaften oder Sporttrainings teil!»

Tobias nickte. Das war ja alles schön und gut, aber musste man gleich ein Buch darüber schreiben? Auch Madison und

Britney schienen Annas Eifer etwas übertrieben zu finden. Zumindest tuschelten und grinsten sie so. Als Tobias Britney ansah, guckte sie jedoch gleich wieder finster.

«Let's go get some food!» Madison said when they arrived at the cafeteria. «I'm sooooo hungry!»

«Me, too,» Tobias said. «What can we get here?»

«You know, burgers, French fries. Oh, and salad if you're vegetarian,» Madison said.

«I'll have a hamburger,» Tobias said. Then he asked: «What are French fries?»

Anna schien nur auf seine Frage gewartet zu haben. «Französisch geröstete Kartoffelstifte», erklärte sie gewichtig. «Auf deutsch: Pommes frites.»

«Ach so», sagte Tobias. Ein bisschen dumm kam er sich vor.

The four of them got burgers, fries, and some drinks: Britney and Madison and Tobias had some coke, Anna had something called root beer.

«What is that?» Tobias asked the two Americans. Madison wanted to answer, but Anna was faster.

«Root beer», begann Anna, «zu Deutsch wörtlich: Wurzelbier. Kein wirkliches Bier, sondern ein Softdrink. Typisch amerikanisch. Schmeckt meiner Meinung nach vorzüglich.»

Sie schob Tobias ihr Glas zum Probieren hin. Er nahm den Pappbecher und die drei Mädchen guckten ihn erwartungsvoll an. Er setzte an, schluckte und verzog dann das Gesicht.

«Das schmeckt ja wie Odol!», sagte er zu Anna und hustete. Diese lächelte säuerlich.

«Did you hear that?» she said to the two American girls. «He just said root beer tastes like mouth wash!»

Madison laughed out loud, and even Britney smiled a little. «I never liked it much either,» Madison agreed. «So what do you like to drink, Tobias?» she asked.

«I like juice or coke a lot. But my favorite drink is coconut and chocolate milkshake. Do you know that?» Tobias answered.

«I love milkshakes!» Madison replied excitedly. «We should take you to the best milkshake-place in the world: there's a *Lundquist's Supershakes* out by the shopping mall. Their shakes are awesome! We can go there this weekend if you like,» and then added, with a glance to her friend, «can't we, Brit?»

«Sure,» Britney mumbled. She looked at her friend. Madison seemed *very* excited.

This was strange. Why was her friend so interested in hanging out with that German idiot? It almost seemed like Madison was starting to actually *like* him!

Als Tobias am Montagabend ins Bett ging, fühlte er sich erschöpft, aber eigentlich ganz zufrieden. Britney strafte ihn zwar immer noch mit Schweigen, aber sonst waren eigentlich alle ganz nett. Na ja, außer Anna vielleicht. Aber Madison schien wirklich cool zu sein, und Milchshake-trinken-Gehen war keine schlechte Idee fürs Wochenende.

Tobias nahm das Programm der Austauschschüler, das Frau Berger ihnen nach dem Unterricht ausgehändigt hatte, in die Hand. Für diese Woche war nicht mehr viel geplant. Alle Schülerinnen und Schüler sollten so viel Zeit wie möglich mit ihren Gastfamilien verbringen und jeden Tag mit in die Schule gehen. «Schön viel Zeit mit Britney also», dachte Tobias und seufzte. Die zweite Woche sah da schon abwechslungsreicher aus. Neben den üblichen Schulbesuchen stand auf dem Programm:

Week 2

Monday

Day Trip to Chicago
German and American students will go to Chicago by bus. We'll see the Sears Tower, Lake Michigan, The Hard Rock Cafe and lots more. There might just be enough time for some shopping on the Miracle Mile!

Wednesday
Day Trip to Six Flags and the Mars Cheese Castle
We will go to the biggest theme park you have ever seen. On our way there, we will stop at the Cheese Castle for souvenirs and some real Wisconsin flavor!

Friday Afternoon
German-American soccer tournament
Call it *Fussball* or soccer – everyone can play!

Friday Night
German-American Barbecue
To celebrate this afternoon's winners, we will have an Oktoberfest-style BBQ with bratwurst, steak, hamburgers, and all your favorite foods!

Das klang doch alles ziemlich gut. Am Montag in die Groß-
stadt, und dieser *Six Flags*-Freizeitpark am Mittwoch klang
auch cool. «Vielleicht gibt's da diese riesigen Loopingbahnen»,
hoffte Tobias. Dann am Freitag Fußball – Tobias grinste in sich
hinein. Da konnte er Britney dann mal vormachen, wie man
richtig «soccer» spielt! Und dann noch eine Grillparty, das war
wirklich nicht verkehrt.

Für die dritte Woche des Austausches gab es nur einen ein-
zigen Eintrag auf dem Programm:

Week 3

Spring Break
Roosevelt High School will be closed.
German students are free to spend time with their host
families, go on family trips etc. There will also be activities
for those students who stay in Appleton. These will be announced later.

Tobias legte das Programm aus der Hand und gähnte. «Hoffentlich heißt das nicht, dass ich mit Familie Summerfield
in den Urlaub fahren muss!», dachte er. Dann knipste er das
Licht aus, zog sich die Decke über den Kopf und schlief sofort
ein.

Kapitel Vierzehn –
Girl Talk ✈

Tuesday, Wednesday and Thursday passed without anything special happening. Britney was busy going to school, then to soccer practice, and at night, she always had to do a lot of homework. Of course Tobias came along wherever she went:

Eight o'clock history: Tobias sat on her left.

Lunch break: Tobias ate his burger across the table from her.

Afternoon Chemistry: Tobias sat on her right.

Homework at night: Tobias read a book on the couch.

And so on.

There was only one exception. Britney had not asked Tobias to come to soccer practice. Madison thought that her friend was acting silly.

«Oh, come on, Brit,» she said to her after practice on Friday. «I think Tobias is *fun*! I can't believe you're still angry at him!»

«And *I* can't believe that you like him!» Britney told her friend. «I still think that comment on girls and soccer was so dumb!»

At this point, Anna joined the conversation. «Many people in Germany think that soccer is a boy's sport,» she said to the two Americans. «A lot of boys play soccer, but not a lot of girls.»

«Really?» Britney said. Madison looked surprised, too.

«Yes,» Anna answered. «I think that Tobias simply doesn't know that soccer is the most popular girl's sport in the world.»

«I'm *sure* he doesn't know!» Britney remarked.

Madison grinned at her friend. «Well,» she said, «let's show him next Friday what we're made of!»

«What's going on on Friday?» Britney asked.

Anna took the three folded pages of paper out of her bag and pointed to the second page. «German-American soccer tournament,» Britney read out loud. Her face lit up. «We are going to *kick his butt*!»

Madison and Anna laughed.

«That's right!» Madison said.

Then she added: «But it's another week until Friday. We should make plans for what we'll do *until then*. How about going to the mall tomorrow? We could get those milkshakes at *Lundquist's*!»

Britney thought for a second. «Sure, why not,» she sighed. «I'm sure it'll be more fun than watching TV with Tobias all day.» She was still pronouncing his name the wrong way.

Madison smiled at her friend. «I'm sure my mom can give us a ride. How about we pick you and *To-bi-as* up at eleven?» As always, Madison tried to say Tobias's name the way he had taught her.

«Alright,» Britney said. «It's a deal.»

Chapter Fifteen –
«*Coole*» Milchshakes ✈

Am Samstagvormittag stiegen Tobias und Britney in den Minivan der Kimballs. Mrs Kimball saß am Steuer, Anna und Madison saßen auf den hinteren Bänken.

«Hey guys, are you ready for some shopping?» Madison greeted them.

«Sure thing,» Britney said. Tobias nodded.

«Do you want to buy anything in particular?» Madison asked. Both Britney and Tobias shook their heads.

«Maybe some postcards,» Tobias said. «For my parents and my grandparents.»

«Anna needs postcards, too,» Madison said. «What else did you want to buy, Anna?»

Erst jetzt sah Tobias, dass Anna, wie so oft, etwas auf ihren Notizblock kritzelte. Diesmal sah ihr Geschreibsel aus wie eine Einkaufsliste. Eine *sehr lange* Einkaufsliste.

«Let's see,» Anna began. «I need postcards and a new film for my camera. I would also like to buy some books, I heard there are some great bookstores at the Fox River Mall. I would like another book about Chicago – mine is already a few years old – and maybe some more informational material about Wisconsin. Do you think I could also get some souvenirs; perhaps a shirt or a cap that says ‹Wisconsin› or ‹Appleton›, or some typical Wisconsin food? And I think I'd like to get some presents for my family. Maybe some candles for my mom, and a calendar for my dad. And I also need –»

«Oooookay,» Madison interrupted Anna and laughed. «Let's start with the postcards.»

After a fifteen minute drive they arrived at Fox River Mall.

«Have a great time! I'll pick you up at five!» Mrs Kimball called after them when they got out of the minivan.

The Fox River Mall was a huge square building surrounded by a huge parking lot. The four of them walked inside, and Anna went straight for the first store. Madison and Britney followed her inside, but Tobias looked around first.

«Das sieht hier aus wie eine riesige überdachte Fußgängerzone», dachte er. Geschäfte jeder erdenklichen Art reihten sich aneinander, und nach den Rolltreppen zu urteilen, die er in einiger Enfernung entdeckte, existierte auch ein zweites Geschoss, in dem es sicher noch mehr Läden gab. Und nach links deutete ein Schild zum *Food Court*. «Da gibt's sicher nachher die Milchshakes!», dachte Tobias. Dann folgte er den Mädchen in das Geschäft.

Drei Stunden später machten sich Tobias, Britney, Madison und Anna, bepackt mit Plastiktüten jeder Größe, auf den Weg zum *Food Court*. Das war eine runde Halle, die einem gemütlichen Innenhof ähnelte: Häuserfassaden und Balkone, unechte Blumenstauden und Bäume zierten die Wände und erinnerten Tobias ein bisschen an seinen letzten Sommerurlaub, den er mit seinen Eltern in Italien verbracht hatte. Auch ansonsten machte der *Food Court* seinem Namen alle Ehre: Überall um sie herum befanden sich Restaurants, und dazwischen ließen sich Dutzende von Menschen das Essen an kleinen Tischen schmecken.

«What do you guys want?» Britney asked. «Milkshakes and ice cream, or some real food? There's Mexican, Chinese, Indian, Italian …»

«I think milkshakes would be great!» Tobias said instantly.

«Sure, I'm *always* up for milkshakes! Isn't that why we came here in the first place?!» Madison said, excited.

«*I* would prefer some *healthy* food today,» Anna said. «Like a salad.»

«Well, that's the great thing about the Food Court,» Britney explained. «We can get food at all these different places, but we can still sit together.»

Anna and Tobias nodded.

«Why don't you get a salad at that Italian place over there, at *Mazzone's*?» Britney suggested to Anna and pointed to her left. «And we can get milkshakes at *Lundquist's*.» She pointed to her right. «And then we can all sit together at one of the tables in the middle of the court.»

Anna and Tobias nodded again.

«Let's go then!» Madison said. «See you in a few minutes, Anna!»

Die Auswahl bei *Lundquist's Supershakes* war riesig, und Tobias fiel es schwer, sich zwischen den unterschiedlichen Eis- und Milchshakesorten zu entscheiden. Britney und Madison wussten sofort, was sie wollten: Madison bestellte einen Shake aus Vanilleeis und Zimt, mit einer großen Portion Sahne und gehackten Nüssen obendrauf. Britney nahm drei Kugeln Eis, auch mit Sahne, verziert mit bunten Zuckerperlen. Dazu bestellte sie noch einen großen Becher Cola. Nach langem Überlegen entschied Tobias sich für den *Double Chocolate Cheesecake Shake*. Er bezahlte und balancierte den riesigen Pappbecher vorsichtig an den Tisch, an dem sich die drei Mädchen niedergelassen hatten.

«That looks great, Tobias! What did you get?» Madison called when he put his paper cup down. «It's the *Double Chocolate Cheesecake Shake,*» Tobias said, «with little pieces of cheesecake, ice cream, and a LOT of chocolate.»

«That sounds really good,» Madison said. «Mine tastes great, too. It's the *Vanilla Cinnamon Walnut Shake.* Do you want to try?»

«Of course!» Tobias said. He grabbed Madison's cup and took a sip. It really *did* taste good.

«I like it!» He said and gave the cup back to Madison. Looking at Anna, he added: «It tastes a lot better than root beer!»

Madison and Britney laughed.

Anna gave him a sour look. «I didn't get root beer today,» she said, sounding a little annoyed. «I got orange juice, because orange juice is healthier. Would you like to try it?»

Tobias shook his head.

«Would you like to try it, Madison?» Anna asked.

«Thanks, I'm cool.» Madison answered.

«Britney, would you like to try my orange juice? It's really good!» Anna kept asking, sounding a little more annoyed.

«I'm cool, Anna, thanks though.»

Now Anna exploded. «Do you all think you're too cool for my orange juice?» she shouted.

Britney and Madison first looked very confused, then they broke out in wild laughter. «No, no, I just meant that –» Britney almost couldn't talk because she was laughing so hard.

«Don't be mad, Anna –» Madison began, but she was also laughing too hard to finish her sentence.

Also war es diesmal *Tobias*, der *Anna* etwas erklären konnte. «‹I'm cool› heißt nur so viel wie ‹I'm fine› oder ‹I'm o.k.›, Anna», sagte er und versuchte, dabei nicht ganz so großspurig zu klingen wie Anna. «Die beiden denken nicht, dass sie zu cool sind, sie möchten einfach nur nicht probieren.»

Anna war dunkelrot angelaufen und zum ersten Mal ziemlich sprachlos. «Oh», murmelte sie nur und stocherte verlegen in ihrem Salat.

«Don't worry, Anna,» Britney said. «Everybody makes mistakes. Remember how Madison and I always said ‹Sie› instead of ‹du›?»

«Yes,» Anna answered. «But …»

«No buts!» Madison said. «Let's drink to making mistakes.

Take your shake, Tobias, and you two, take your coke and your juice – here's to *cool* mistakes!»

«Cheers!» Tobias shouted.

«Prost!» Britney said, laughing.

Anna was still a little quiet, but she was smiling, too.

Kapitel Sechzehn –
The Big City ✈

On Monday morning at eight o'clock, all the German students and their American partners were getting on a bus to go to Chicago. The bus was a typical American school bus: it was bright yellow and had «Roosevelt High School» written on the side. The two teachers, Mrs Mayers and Mrs Berger, were there, too. They were counting their students before leaving.

«Forty-eight … forty-nine … fifty. Everybody's here!» Mrs Mayers called to her colleague. Mrs Berger nodded and said something to the driver. He started the engine and the group began their journey.

Tobias hatte einen Platz neben Björn, einem Jungen aus seiner Parallelklasse, ergattert. Die beiden unterhielten sich über die letzten Tage und ihre Austauschpartner.

«James und ich waren gestern bei einem American-Football-Spiel, das war richtig cool. Und am Samstag haben wir mit seinen Freunden Bowling gespielt. James ist echt cool, und seine Freunde auch», berichtete Björn begeistert. Dann fragte er: «Bei wem wohnst du eigentlich?»

Tobias deutete vage hinter sich, wo Britney neben Madison saß. «Bei der da, mit den braunen Haaren», sagte er.

Björn grinste. «Und, wie ist die so?»

«Na ja», sagte Tobias nur, «es geht.»

Björn lachte.

«Ich glaube, mit James hatte ich echt Glück», sagte er dann. «Nur eins ist komisch – er kann meinen Namen überhaupt nicht aussprechen. Er gibt sich echt Mühe, aber er nennt mich immer ‹Biii-dschorn› oder so ähnlich.» Björn versuchte, seinen Austauschpartner nachzumachen.

Jetzt lachte Tobias. «Britney nennt mich auch immer ‹Tobei-äs›», erzählte er Björn. «Aber», fügte er hinzu, «ich glaube, sie gibt sich auch extra keine Mühe.»

«Mädchen eben!», sagte Björn grinsend. «Aber wenigstens sieht sie gar nicht mal so schlecht aus.»

Tobias sah ihn überrascht an. Von dieser Seite hatte er die ganze Sache noch gar nicht betrachtet. Britney sah wirklich ganz gut aus, aber vor lauter Zickerei hatte er das gar nicht mehr bemerkt.

Meanwhile, Madison and Britney were discussing what to do with their free time in Chicago. «It might be fun to go window shopping, but I'm pretty sure I don't want to buy anything,» said Britney.

«Me neither. Everyone says the *Miracle Mile* is great for looking around, but much too expensive. But did you know there's a *Niketown* there? That's a great store for sports clothes. Maybe we can look at soccer shoes.»

Britney leaned in and whispered to Madison: «I don't think my exchange brother would want to watch us try out soccer shoes.»

«What?» Madison whispered back, «I actually thought he could come with us,» she continued with a playful smile.

«No way! I don't want him to go!» Britney was still whispering. «He thinks only boys can play soccer, and he probably also thinks that girls should only cook and play with dolls.»

«Oh, relax.» Madison was now talking quietly, but the background noise on the bus was loud enough that only Britney could hear her. «Remember? Anna said that girls just don't play soccer much in Germany. He probably just didn't know.»

«Still, he doesn't have to be such an idiot,» Britney replied.

«Britney, that was *one* time. It was really not that bad. And I think he was probably joking. Besides, he's …,» Madison hesitated.

«What?» Britney asked.

«You know, a lot of the other girls are jealous of you for getting him as your exchange partner.»

«What?» Britney repeated. «What in the world are you talking about?»

«Janie, Payton, Emily, they all agree with me.»

«Agree with you on what?» Britney inquired, skeptical.

Madison went back down to whispering volume. «*He's cute.*

If you just looked at him for a second without thinking about that stupid soccer comment, you'd see it.»

To underline her statement, Madison got out her cell phone and hit a few buttons. «Look, I got this message from Janie yesterday.» She said and handed the phone to Britney. On the display it said:

> Are U going to the BBQ on
> friday? i want to see brit's
> german guy – he's soooo cute!
> janie

Britney was surprised, but she still didn't want to believe it.

«Whatever,» she said.

«Come on. It's not healthy to be so unforgiving. Just relax and try to be nice to him. Give it a chance.»

Britney thought about Madison's diplomacy for a moment. Tobias hadn't really said or done anything bad since the soccer comment. Why was she still so angry about one little thing? And maybe he *was* cute …

«All right,» Britney heard herself say. «But what am I supposed to do?»

«Just relax. Be yourself. Forget about the stupid comment. It's not worth it to always think about it,» Madison said.

«You're right,» Britney said after a little pause. «O.k. I'll give Tobias another chance.»

Die meiste Zeit ging die Fahrt durch Weideland und Felder. Tobias und Björn sahen Ortsnamen wie Oshkosh, Fon Du

Lac, West Bend und Germantown. Bei dem letzten Straßen-
schild verrenkten sich die beiden die Hälse, um einen Blick
auf die Stadt zu werfen. Doch alles, was man vom Bus aus von
Germantown sehen konnte, waren drei Tankstellen und eine
Autoschlange vor einem Fast-Food-Restaurant. Als sie durch
Milwaukee fuhren, gab es endlich mehr zu sehen.

«Milwaukee looks so big! It must be bigger than … Hamburg!», sagte Björn zu der Amerikanerin, die auf der anderen
Seite des Ganges saß. Doch bevor sie ihm eine Antwort geben
konnte, tauchte Annas Gesicht hinter ihr auf. «Milwaukee ist
nicht größer als Hamburg», klärte sie Björn auf. «In Milwaukee leben circa 650 000 Menschen, in Hamburg dagegen fast
zwei Millionen.» Wie immer klang sie, als würde sie direkt aus
einem ihrer zahlreichen Stadtführer vorlesen.

«Äh, ja, danke für die aufschlussreiche Information», sagte
Björn spöttisch.

Als sie endlich Chicago erreicht hatten, waren die deutschen
Schülerinnen und Schüler begeistert. Tobias dachte, er hätte
vom Flughafen aus schon einiges von der Stadt gesehen, doch
jetzt merkte er, dass er sich geirrt hatte. Das wahre Chicago
war viel größer, als er sich vorgestellt hatte, ein Wolkenkratzer
höher als der andere. Der Bus fuhr über Brücken und durch
Tunnel, immer auf mehrspurigen Straßen im dichtgedrängten
Verkehr. Als sie den Lake Shore Drive erreicht hatten, war Tobias sprachlos. Auf der einen Seite des Busses lag Lake Michigan, ein See so groß, dass man ihn leicht für ein Meer halten

konnte. Auf der anderen Seite reihten sich riesige Hochhäuser aus Glas, Stahl und Stein aneinander, so weit das Auge reichte.

«Welcome to Chicago!» said Mrs Mayers over the bus loudspeaker. «… the capital of the Midwest, and America's third largest city. Only New York and Los Angeles are bigger than Chicago.»

Some pieces of paper were being passed around the bus.

«I'm handing out today's schedule,» continued Mrs Mayers. «We're going to do our best to stick to it, but we need everyone's cooperation. I want each of you to find your exchange partner and make sure that he or she is with us at all times.» Right then, Tobias felt someone tap on his shoulder, he turned around to see Britney. She waved at him through the gap between the seats.

Tobias war verwundert über diese freundliche Geste. «Was ist denn jetzt los?», dachte er, lächelte dann aber kurz in ihre Richtung.

«Now, we're going to start by going to the top of the Sears Tower, so you can get a sense of how big the city really is,» said Mrs Mayers over the loudspeaker. «We'll be there in just a few minutes, and after the tower we'll walk over to the *Hard Rock Café* for lunch. Is everyone ready?»

«YES! READY!» Tobias heard Björn scream louder than anyone else. As Tobias laughed, he heard Britney laugh a little too.

After a few more minutes of driving through the mountainous buildings, they arrived at the foot of the Sears Tower. Britney looked up when she got out of the bus. It looked like a black road made of glass, going straight up into outer space. She followed the group into the basement where they stood in line to wait for the elevator to the top. Tobias leaned over to her and asked: «Have you ever been to the top before?»

«No,» she said. «My parents took me to the top of the Hancock building once, but it's not as tall.»

They got into the elevator together with about fifteen other students.

«Why didn't you come here?» Tobias asked.

«The lines were too long,» Britney answered.

Suddenly, Britney covered her ears with her hands. «Ooh, my ears just popped from the pressure change. Did you feel that?» she asked.

Tobias replied: «Yes, I just felt it. I thought that only happened on airplanes.»

«It's a very tall building. You may want to try yawning,» Anna answered before Britney could say anything.

«Thanks,» Britney said to Anna, then turned to Tobias and rolled her eyes. Tobias smiled back. Britney thought it was funny that Tobias also had enough of Anna.

When the elevator doors opened on the top floor, all that they could see was blue sky. They walked towards the windows and saw the gigantic city rise up below them.

«Wow!» Tobias said as he looked down. The cars and trucks looked like little toys.

«Come here, Tobias,» said Britney. She actually pronounced

his name correctly this time. He walked to her. «Pretty cool, huh?» She was looking out over Lake Michigan.

«You can always tell which way you're going in Chicago because the lake is east.» Britney said as she pointed out the window. «So do you know where we came from?»

Tobias tried to remember a map of the United States. He was pretty sure he knew, so he turned left and pointed toward the northern window. «That way?»

«That's right,» said Britney. «And if you look that way …»

«Is that Milwaukee?» Tobias could see a small blue shadow from the Milwaukee skyline just on the horizon.

«It's almost a hundred miles away … I mean, about 150 kilometers.»

«Nicht schlecht!» Tobias said, sounding impressed. Britney didn't know why Tobias had answered in German, but she understood what he meant right away. «Ja, das ist nicht schlecht!» she said and gave him a big smile.

Tobias und Britney kamen als Letzte wieder auf der Straße an. Die Hälfte der Gruppe hatte sich schon mit Frau Berger auf den Weg zum *Hard Rock Cafe* gemacht. Jetzt setzte sich auch die zweite Gruppe mit Mrs Mayers in Bewegung. Tobias, Britney und Madison blieben etwas hinter den anderen zurück. Madison erzählte den beiden, was sie gerade von den anderen Amerikanern erfahren hatte. «Did you know that there is a really famous *McDonald's* near the *Hard Rock Cafe*?»

«Why would a *McDonald's* restaurant be famous?», fragte Britney.

«I think it's just really big and full of neon lights», antwortete Madison.

«Really? That sounds cooler than the *Hard Rock Cafe*», schaltete sich Tobias ein. Er war ohnehin kein großer Fan von Hard-Rock-Musik, und das Essen bei McDonald's schmeckte ihm besonders gut.

«Let's go to that *McDonald's*, then!», schlug Britney vor. «Does anyone know where it is exactly?»

Tobias schüttelte den Kopf. Madison sagte: «I'm not sure, but I think it's only a few minutes from here, down that street over there.»

«Let's go!», rief Tobias.

Anstatt den anderen ins *Hard Rock Cafe* zu folgen, machten sich Tobias, Madison und Britney also auf die Suche nach Chicagos berühmtem *McDonald's*.

Chapter Seventeen –
Wo bitte geht's zu McDonald's? ✈

Sie hatten schon vier große Kreuzungen überquert und waren gerade zum zweiten Mal in eine Seitenstraße abgebogen, als Madison vorschlug, jemanden nach dem Weg zu fragen. Britney sprach einen Mann an, der ihnen tatsächlich eine Wegbeschreibung geben konnte. Die drei liefen wieder los, doch nach ein paar Minuten konnten sie sich nicht mehr an die Beschreibung des Mannes erinnern und standen wieder suchend an einer Straßenecke. Madison und Britney guckten ziemlich hilflos drein.

Erst jetzt wurde Tobias bewusst, dass die beiden sich in Chicago wirklich genauso wenig auskannten wie er.

Häuserschluchten und Kreuzungen glichen hier einander wie ein Ei dem anderen. Überall um sie herum waren Menschen: Einige schlenderten gemütlich vorüber und studierten interessiert die vielen Schaufenster, die meisten jedoch hasteten an den Läden vorbei, ohne sie eines Blickes zu würdigen. Auf den Straßen drängten sich dicht an dicht die Autoschlangen.

«I think we've lost our way,» Britney said, worried. «And we can't see the lake from here, so we have no idea where east is.»

Madison looked a little scared, too. «We've been walking around for ...» she checked her watch, «twenty-five minutes! This is impossible!»

«What should we do?» Britney asked.

«Let's ask somebody else where we are,» Tobias suggested.

Britney nodded. «I guess it's the only thing we can do.» She looked for someone she could ask. When she spotted a friendly-looking middle-aged woman, Britney walked over to her and described their situation. Tobias could see the woman nod and point to her right.

Also bogen Tobias, Britney und Madison nach rechts ab und folgten dieser Straße. Wieder überquerten sie zwei Kreuzungen. Doch von *McDonald's* war immer noch weit und breit nichts zu sehen. Tobias fühlte sich ziemlich mulmig. Sie waren schon weit über eine halbe Stunde unterwegs und hatten keine Ahnung, wo sie sich befanden. Was, wenn sie nicht rechtzeitig zum Bus zurückfänden? Wenn er jetzt in Deutschland wäre, könnte er einfach jemanden anrufen, aber hier in Amerika funktionierte sein Handy natürlich nicht. Und er wusste, dass Britney ihr Telefon nicht auf den Ausflug mitgenommen hatte. Aber was war mit Madison? Sie müsste doch ihr Handy haben!

«Madison, do you have your handy?» Tobias asked.

«My what?» Madison said.

«Her what?» Britney said.

«Her handy. We can call someone and ask for help!»

«Handy?» Madison still sounded confused. «What do you mean?»

«Your telephone!» Tobias said impatiently.

«Oh, you mean my *cell phone*!» Madison said and smiled. «Is ‹handy› the German word for it?»

«Yes, we call … cell phones … handies,» Tobias said slowly.

Er war ein bisschen verwirrt. Er hatte immer gedacht, «Handy» wäre ein englisches Wort. War es aber offensichtlich nicht. Gerade war allerdings nicht der richtige Zeitpunkt, um über Vokabeln nachzudenken.

«Do you have your cell phone?» he asked again.

Britney understood what Tobias was thinking. «Get out

your cell phone, Madison, we can call my parents and ask for directions,» she said to her friend.

«That's a really good idea!» Madison agreed.

She put her hand into the right pocket of her pants, than into the left pocket. Then she checked the pockets of her jacket. No cell phone. «That's strange. Where is my phone?» she mumbled.

«It must be in your backpack!» Britney said.

Madison opened her backpack and went through all her stuff. She even checked the little secret pocket on the inside. No cell phone.

«Damn it!» Madison shouted and kicked a trash can with her right foot. Clearly, she was more angry than scared now. «I left the stupid phone on the bus!»

«Oh no!» Tobias sighed.

«What are we going to do *now*?» Britney asked.

«Maybe we can try to walk back. Let's just turn around and try to trace our steps.» Madison suggested.

The other two nodded. They didn't have a better idea.

Tobias wollte sich gerade umdrehen, um den beiden Mädchen zu folgen, da fiel sein Blick auf eine Frau, die auf der anderen Seite der Straße entlanghastete. Sie trug eine hellblaue Jacke und hatte kurze, blonde Haare. Tobias stutzte: Das war doch seine Lehrerin, Frau Berger!

«Hallo», rief er, so laut er konnte, «Frau Berger!»

Einige Passanten schauten ihn verwundert an, doch die Frau

auf der anderen Straßenseite reagierte nicht. Es war wohl einfach zu laut. Tobias konnte sie nur noch von hinten sehen, und sie entfernte sich immer weiter. Jetzt hieß es, schnell zu handeln!

«There!» Tobias shouted to Britney and Madison. «That's Mrs Berger over there! We have to stop her!»

«Where?» Madison said.

Tobias pointed at the woman, but she was too far away. «Let's follow her!» Tobias yelled. «Quick!»

Die drei spurteten die Straße hinunter, zwischen den vielen Menschen hindurch. Sie durften Frau Berger jetzt nicht aus den Augen verlieren! Und sie mussten unbedingt auf die andere Straßenseite gelangen! Um auf die nächste grüne Ampel zu warten, war keine Zeit. Unter einem lauten Hupkonzert schlängelten sich die drei durch die Autoreihen. Madison und Britney waren schon auf der anderen Straßenseite, als Tobias stolperte. Er taumelte vorwärts, Bremsen quietschten – gerade noch rechtzeitig konnte er sich fangen und auf den Bürgersteig springen. Hinter sich hörte er den Fahrer des Wagens aus dem geöffneten Fenster schimpfen.

«Are you o.k.?» Britney asked.

Tobias nodded quickly. «Where is Mrs Berger?» he asked.

«There, I can still see her!» Madison shouted. «Let's go!»

The three of them started running again. The woman was still far away. And there was another traffic light between her and them. They would have to be really fast.

An der nächsten Kreuzung war das Glück auf ihrer Seite: Die Ampel sprang in dem Moment auf Grün, als die drei sie erreichten. So schnell sie konnten liefen sie auf die andere Seite. Aber wo war Frau Berger? An der nächsten Ampel schien sie nicht zu warten, und auch auf der anderen Straßenseite konnte Tobias sie nicht erkennen. Auch die beiden Mädchen schauten sich suchend um.

«Where did she go?» Britney asked, out of breath.

They looked all over. Where *was* Mrs Berger?

«I think we lost her,» Madison said miserably.

«I can't believe it!» Britney said. «She disappeared!»

Tobias climbed up on a bench and looked around from there. And it was from there that he saw her: Mrs Berger had just come out of the store in front of them. Tobias spotted her light blue jacket and her blonde hair right away. Frau Berger was now carrying a brown paper bag, and she was starting to walk away from them again.

«Wait here! I'll catch her,» he shouted to the girls and ran after the woman.

Tobias brauchte nur noch etwa fünfzig Meter, dann hatte er Frau Berger erreicht. «Frau Berger!», rief er und klopfte der Frau von hinten auf die Schulter.

Die Frau drehte sich um.

Zum ersten Mal sah Tobias ihr Gesicht und konnte es nicht fassen: Diese Frau war nicht Frau Berger. Von nahem hatte sie noch nicht mal *Ähnlichkeit* mit Frau Berger. Sie waren die ganze Zeit hinter einer völlig fremden Frau hergelaufen!

«Are you alright, dear?», sagte die Frau nun zu ihm.

«Yes, ääh … I'm sorry …», murmelte Tobias verlegen. Dann drehte er auf dem Absatz um. «Bloß weg!», dachte er.

Madison and Britney had watched everything. When they saw Tobias' face, they knew they would have to cheer him up.

«It was worth a try, Tobias,» Britney said in a friendly voice.

«I thought she was Mrs Berger, too!» Madison added.

Tobias felt very embarrassed, but it helped a little that the girls weren't laughing at him.

«Let's sit down and think about what to do next,» Britney suggested. Madison nodded, and the three sat down on the bench.

Britney checked her watch. «We've been lost for more than an hour!» she said, worried.

«How long was the lunch break supposed to be?» Madison asked.

«Exactly one hour,» Tobias said tiredly.

«Oh no,» Madison said. «Everybody is probably already back on the bus.»

«Do you think they'll leave without us?» Britney said, sounding nervous.

Madison shrugged her shoulders. «I hope not!» she answered.

Britney und Madison schienen mit ihrem Latein am Ende. Auch Tobias wusste nicht, was sie als Nächstes probieren könnten. «Jetzt hilft nur noch ein Wunder!», dachte er bei sich. In Gedanken versunken saßen die drei auf der Bank und starrten auf den Verkehr, der an ihnen vorbeirauschte. Darum bekam auch keiner der drei mit, dass eine Person sich ihnen von hinten näherte. Als sie sie ansprach, fuhren Madison, Britney und Tobias zusammen.

«Hey!», rief die Person gut gelaunt. «Seid ihr fertig für die Stadtrundfahrt?»

Vor ihnen stand Anna. Bestens gelaunt und wie immer mit einem dicken Reiseführer in der Hand. Tobias hätte nicht gedacht, dass er einmal so glücklich sein würde, Anna zu sehen. Auch Britney und Madison waren vor Freude aufgesprungen.

«I'm so happy to see you!» Madison shouted and gave Anna a big hug.

«We're so glad you're here!» Britney said happily as she hugged the German girl, too.

Anna was surprised. «Why are you so excited?» she asked. «We've only been apart for one hour!»

«But we got lost!» Britney explained.

«How on earth did you get here anyway?» Madison asked.

Anna still looked surprised. «How did I get *here*?»

«Wir haben keine Ahnung, wo wir sind!», mischte sich Tobias ein. «Kannst du in deinem Stadtführer nachgucken, wie wir wieder zurück zum Bus kommen?»

Anna guckte von Tobias zu Britney und von Britney zu Madison und dann wieder zu Tobias. Sie grinste von einem Ohr zum anderen. Dann nahm sie ihren Stadtführer und schlug den Stadtplan von Chicago auf. Tobias sah, dass die ganze Stadt wie ein riesiges Schachbrett angeordnet war: Die Straßen liefen alle parallel zueinander und wurden in den gleichen Abständen von anderen Straßen im immer gleichen Winkel gekreuzt. Kein Wunder, dass sie die Übersicht verloren hatten!

Anna held the map so Tobias, Madison and Britney could see it. She pointed somewhere on the map and said: «This is where we are.» The three nodded.

«And do you want to know where the bus is?» Anna asked, smiling. The three nodded again.

But instead of pointing to the map again, Anna closed the book. With a big smile, she looked from Tobias, to Britney, to Madison. The three looked back at her expectantly. Then, Anna turned around and pointed behind the bench on which the other three were sitting. «The bus is *right there*!!» she said, bursting with laughter.

Tobias fuhr herum. Da, auf der anderen Straßenseite, stand der Bus. Er konnte es nicht fassen. Sie hatten direkt neben dem Bus gesessen! Und sie waren eine Stunde lang im Kreis gelaufen!

Madison and Britney looked like they didn't know if they should laugh or cry.

«This is crazy! *Unbelievable!*» Madison shouted. «We are such idiots!»

Britney shook her head in complete surprise. «I can't *believe* it! Tobias, can you believe this? We walked around in circles!»

Tobias konnte es tatsächlich nicht glauben. Obwohl er sich auch ziemlich blöd vorkam, überwog jetzt die Erleichterung, dass die abenteuerliche Suche endlich zu Ende war. Und ganz am Rande registrierte er, dass Britney seinen Namen schon wieder richtig ausgesprochen hatte.

Wieder im Bus erzählte er Björn – der jetzt ein Hard-Rock-Café-T-Shirt trug und Tobias von seinem leckeren Essen vorschwärmte – von seiner misslungenen Mittagspause. Björn konnte sich kaum halten vor Lachen. Er lachte so laut, dass Frau Berger, die jetzt die Schüler zählte, stehen blieb und sich nach dem Grund seiner Freude erkundigte.

«Es ist nichts Interessantes! Ich habe Björn nur eine witzige Geschichte erzählt!», warf Tobias hastig ein.

«Das muss ja eine besonders gute Geschichte gewesen sein!», sagte sie mit einem Blick auf Madison und Britney, die wieder hinter den beiden Jungen saßen und sich das Grinsen ebenfalls nicht verkneifen konnten.

«Did you like the story that Tobias told Björn?» Mrs Berger asked the girls. «Oh yeah!» Madison said, smiling.

And, with an even bigger smile, Britney added: «What I always wanted to tell you, Mrs Berger, I really, *really* like your blue jacket! It looks great with your blonde hair!»

Frau Berger wollte sich eigentlich für dieses nette Kompliment bedanken, doch gegen den neuen Lachanfall, den Britneys Bemerkung bei den vieren ausgelöst hatte, kam sie nicht an. Sie lächelte über das seltsame Verhalten ihrer Schüler und konzentrierte sich dann wieder aufs Zählen.

Kapitel Achtzehn –
Six Flags, Home of the Penny Trick ✈

Auf der Fahrt zur Schule am nächsten Morgen betrachtete Tobias die Gebäude und Straßen von Appleton, die an ihnen vorüberzogen. Nach dem Tag in Chicago erschien ihm die Stadt jetzt richtig klein. Mr Summerfield, der am Steuer des Buick saß, riss ihn aus seinen Gedanken.

«So you two must be *exhausted* from all this riding around on the bus yesterday. Why couldn't you stay at a hotel in Chicago?»

Tobias hatte das Gefühl, dass Mr Summerfield mehr mit sich selbst redete als mit Britney oder ihm. Vielleicht lag das aber auch nur daran, dass er von dem Ausflug gestern tatsächlich noch sehr müde war. Deshalb war er erleichtert, als Britney die Frage ihres Vaters beantwortete.

«Maybe a hotel would have been too expensive?»

Mr Summerfield laughed a little. «Well, I don't think that's it. All this bus time costs a lot more than a hotel would. I think it's simply because many parents didn't want you kids to spend a lot of time in Chicago.»

«What do you mean?» asked Britney.

Mr Summerfield continued: «Some parents think that you would get lost in Chicago because it's a big city.» He laughed. «They think you're little children that can't take care of themselves!»

Jetzt erwiderte Britney nichts. Tobias sah, dass sie angestrengt aus dem Seitenfenster schaute und sich Mühe gab, nicht laut loszulachen. Auch Tobias hielt lieber weiter den Mund. Schließlich wollte er auf keinen Fall verraten, dass sie sich gestern *tatsächlich* verlaufen hatten.

However, Mr Summerfield didn't notice anything. He continued: «But you were just fine yesterday! You were in a nice part of Chicago; you stayed with the group; nothing happened. But some parents can be so paranoid.»

«Yeah, I think you're right, Dad,» Britney said, still looking out the window. She was relieved to see that they had reached the school.

«Well anyway, here we are. Have a good time, you two, and don't get lost in that ‹dangerous› theme park!!» Mr Summerfield said and laughed about his own joke. Britney and Tobias quickly jumped out of the car as soon as it stopped.

«Bye,» Britney said to her dad.

«Thanks, bye,» Tobias said as he shut the door.

He and Britney both walked slowly towards the rest of the exchange group and their waiting bus as the Buick drove away. Tobias immediately turned to Britney.

«Does your Dad know that we got lost in Chicago?» he asked.

Britney had an excited smile on her face as she turned back to him. «No way. There's no way he could have known. I had a hard time not laughing in the car, though.»

«Oh, Gott sei Dank.» Tobias war erleichtert. Mr Summerfield musste von dieser peinlichen Geschichte wirklich nichts erfahren.

«What does that mean? ‹Thank God›, right? You are *totally* right!!» She started laughing.

Tobias could feel that she was laughing *with* him, and not *at* him, so he started laughing, too.

«Yes, thank God he doesn't know.» Tobias agreed.

They now had a secret to keep from Britney's parents. Tobias felt like they were partners in crime as they climbed aboard the bus for the trip to *Six Flags*.

Die Busfahrt in Richtung Süden war der vom Vortag ziemlich ähnlich. Tobias saß neben Björn, hinter ihnen saßen Britney und Madison. Heute aber unterhielten sich die vier, und die Zeit schien viel schneller zu vergehen. Alle waren überrascht, als sich die Fahrt verlangsamte und Mrs Mayers über Lautsprecher ihren ersten Stopp ankündigte.

«O.k., everyone, we're going to take a little break at the *Mars Cheese Castle*. This is one of the best places for the Germans to buy Wisconsin souvenirs. It's also a good place to get some snacks, because the food at *Six Flags* is really expensive.»

«AND, they don't have cheese curds there», fügte Madison hinzu. «*Six Flags* is in Illinois, and I heard they're not allowed to sell cheese curds outside of Wisconsin.»

«Yeah, let's get some cheese curds here», stimmte Britney begeistert zu, als sie gemeinsam aus dem Bus stiegen. Björn und Tobias guckten sich ratlos an. Sie hatten keine Ahnung, was diese «Cheese Curds» sein sollten. Britney hatte die Blicke der Jungen bemerkt.

«It's a Wisconsin delicacy, you'll see», sagte sie nur.

Das *Cheese Castle* erinnerte Tobias eher an eine große Tankstelle als an ein Schloss. Drinnen stapelten sich Souvenirs in den Regalen, die alle mit Käse zu tun hatten: riesige Schaumstoff-Goudas, T-Shirts, Mützen und Jacken mit Käseaufdruck. Tobias entdeckte sogar einen kleinen Haufen Fußbälle, die wie Käse aussahen. Daneben lag ein viel größerer Berg aus seltsam eiförmigen Bällen. Vor ihnen blieb Tobias stehen.

«What's this?» he asked Madison.

«Footballs,» she answered right away. Then she saw Tobias' confused look. «For American Football.»

Tobias schlug sich vor die Stirn. «Natürlich!» Da war er seit fast zwei Wochen in Amerika, und vor lauter *Soccer* hatte er den *American Football* fast vergessen.

«My dad likes to watch football more than soccer,» Madison said. «Do you see all this green and gold stuff over here?» She pointed to the shelves at her right. They were packed with t-shirts, footballs, posters, helmets and lots of other collectibles. Everything was green and gold.

«We're in Wisconsin, so everyone loves the *Green Bay Packers*. That's the name of the football team here. And green and gold are their colors.»

Tobias nodded, interested.

«Yeah, everybody is *crazy* about the *Green Bay Packers*,» Madison continued. «I think soccer is so much cooler, but no one cares. It's all *Packers, Packers, Packers,* football, football, football.»

Tobias smiled.

Then Britney came up from behind them. «I found the cheese curds and I got two bags for us to share.» She held up two plastic bags filled with finger-sized pieces of what Tobias hoped was just cheese.

Back on the bus, Britney opened up the first bag, and offered the cheese curds to Tobias and Björn. «Try some.»

Tobias took one out of the bag and ate it. It tasted like cheese, but his teeth made a squeaky sound as he chewed.

«Pretty good, huh?» Britney asked.

«Uhm, yes!» Tobias said quickly.

But in reality, he just thought this Wisconsin specialty tasted a little funny.

Als sie den Freizeitpark erreichten, waren beide Tüten Cheese Curds geleert. Tobias und Björn hatten sich zurückgehalten, doch Britney und Madison hatten mit umso mehr Appetit gegessen. Sie kletterten zusammen mit den anderen aus dem Bus, und Mrs Mayers machte die nächste Ankündigung.

«All right everyone, before we go in, you each get thirty dollars from us. We don't want you to go hungry or die of thirst. But make sure to use the money wisely! Everything is really expensive here at *Six Flags*. The rides are free, but everything else costs a *lot* of money.»

«Thirty dollars! Not bad!», staunte Tobias, als er den Umschlag öffnete, den Mrs Mayers ihm gegeben hatte.

«Let's buy something really cold to drink when we're inside», schlug Britney vor.

Nachdem sie am Parkeingang ein paar Minuten Schlange gestanden hatten, machten Britney, Tobias, Björn, Anna und Madison sich zusammen auf die Suche nach kalten Getränken. Das erste Restaurant, das sie entdeckten, war ein Wildwest-Saloon mit dem Namen *The Waterin' Hole*. Der Mann und die Frau hinter der Theke trugen beide Cowboyhüte und altmodische Lederwesten, doch die Bestellungen tippten sie in nagelneue Computerkassen mit Flachbildschirmen. Die Getränke und Speisen, die das *Waterin' Hole* anbot, standen mit schnörkeliger Schrift an einer Tafel an der Wand.

«5.50 dollars for a smoothie??!!», rief Britney entsetzt.

«Yeah, and 3.50 dollars for a bottle of water!», fügte Björn hinzu.

«That's *so* expensive!» stöhnte Anna.

«Let's go find something cheaper», schlug Madison vor.

Tobias fand auch, dass die Getränke viel zu teuer waren. Andererseits hatte er ziemlichen Durst nach den langen Fahrt und den klebrigen Cheese Curds ...

«I don't think that we will find anything cheaper here», sagte Britney, während Tobias noch nachdachte.

«The bubbler is cheaper!», warf Madison ein. «It's free.»

«Bubbler?», fragten Tobias und Björn wie aus einem Mund.

«Yeah, the drinking fountain. They have them near the bathrooms», antwortete Madison.

«That sounds good.» Björn trat aus der Schlange für die Getränke heraus. Er wollte gerne mit Madison einen «Bubbler» suchen.

Britney zögerte. «I don't know. I'd rather sit down and have a real drink than just a sip of water outside the bathrooms. I want to stay at the *Waterin' Hole*.»

Tobias fand Britneys Idee weitaus besser als Madisons. Überhaupt schien es Tobias, als ob Britney und er in der letzten Zeit ziemlich oft einer Meinung gewesen waren.

«I would like to buy a drink, too,» he said. «They gave us thirty dollars, we can afford a nice drink here!»

«O. k.,» Madison said to Britney. «How about you and Tobias stay here and we'll meet you later. Björn, Anna and I will find a bubbler and go on some rides. You can call my cell phone when you want to find us.»

«That sounds good.» Britney said.

Also machten sich Madison, Björn und Anna auf die Suche nach einem Wasserspender, während Tobias und Britney sich im *Waterin' Hole* für ein Getränk anstellten.

Beide bestellten einen Smoothie für $ 5.50.

Während sie das eiskalte Getränk durch ihre Strohhalme schlürften, betrachteten sie die Wildwasserbahn, die gleich neben dem Restaurant lag. Tobias war begeistert von dem etwa 30 Meter hohen Wasserfall, von dem die kleinen Boote stürzten. Die Menschen in den Booten kreischten vor Vergnügen, und niemand störte sich daran, völlig durchnässt aus den Booten zu steigen.

«Do you want to go on that ride first?» Britney asked.

«Yes!» Tobias answered excitedly.

«O.k.!» Britney agreed. «And after that, we can go on *The Drop*.»

«What's *The Drop*?» Tobias asked.

Britneys Erklärung war ziemlich lang und kompliziert, aber Tobias verstand so viel: Bei dem *Drop* schien es sich um ein Gerät zu handeln, bei dem man erst zehn Stockwerke hochgezogen und dann mit vollem Tempo fallen gelassen wurde. Er nickte begeistert.

«I want to show you a trick on *The Drop*!» Britney added.

«O.k., but only if it is not too dangerous!» Tobias joked.

«Oh, shut up, ‹Dad›!» lachte Britney und gab ihm einen freundschaftlichen Stoß in die Seite. Dann stellten sie sich in die Schlange für die Wildwasserbahn. Weit vor ihnen sahen sie Madison und Björn.

«Should we call them?», fragte Tobias.

«No, they're too far ahead. They won't hear us unless we really scream», antwortete Britney.

Tobias suddenly noticed that he didn't really want to call out to Madison and Björn anyway. It was fun to be alone with Britney! The same was true for her: Britney didn't mind at all that their other friends were so far away from them, and that she was alone with Tobias.

They talked about all sorts of things as they waited in line. Britney shared gossip about some of the teachers at Roosevelt, Tobias told stories about his school in Germany. They had a great time and they were on the boat before they knew it.

Das «Boot» war in Wirklichkeit ein ziemlich breites Fahrgestell, das wie in einer Achterbahn auf Schienen gezogen wurde. Tobias und Britney quetschten sich nebeneinander in eine Sitzreihe. Sobald sie saßen, senkte sich ein Arm aus Metall vor ihnen und rastete in die Halterung ein. Das Boot setzte sich in Bewegung. Jetzt gab es kein Zurück.

«Ooh, this is the scariest part. I always want to jump off right now,» said Britney.

«Me, too,» Tobias said. Both were holding as tight as they could to the safety bar in front of them.

«But you have been on this ride before, right?» Tobias asked.

«Uhmm, actually, no,» Britney said. «I was on a different water ride here, but never this one ... Oh boy! ... Here we go!»

Das Boot hatte den höchsten Punkt der Rampe erreicht und hing für einige Sekunden bewegungslos an der Spitze des Wasserfalls. 30 Meter über dem Erdboden.

Zuerst bewegten sie sich nur ganz langsam. Tobias warf Britney einen Blick zu und sah, dass sie ihre Augen fest zugekniffen hatte. Einen Moment lang schaute er sie noch an, dann fiel das Boot mit einem lauten Quietschen nach vorn. Alle fingen an zu kreischen.

Tobias fühlte sich für einen Moment wie schwerelos, als das Boot in die Tiefe stürzte. Nur zwei Sekunden später schlug es wieder auf dem Wasser auf. Eine riesige Welle schwappte über Tobias und Britney hinweg.

«Ohmygod! That's cooolllldddd!», schrie Britney. Auch Tobias war von oben bis unten klitschnass. Sie sah ihn an und lachte. «I guess we don't need to spend any more money on cold drinks.»

«Brrr ...», war die einzige Antwort, die Tobias geben konnte. Britney lachte noch lauter, und auch Tobias musste grinsen.

As the boat landed and they climbed off, Tobias felt the sun warming and drying him. The shock of the ice cold water quickly went away. In fact, Tobias had forgotten all about it by the time they got back out into the rest of the park.

«Wow, that was pretty cool, huh?» Britney asked.

«Yes, very cool, and very cold,» Tobias replied.

«Are you ready to go on *The Drop*?»

«As long as there is no water there.»

«Ha ha. Don't worry, I think that's the last of our water rides for today,» Britney laughed. «Let's go.» She started walking as she pointed to a round tower. «It's this way.»

Rund um diesen Turm wurden Menschen in ziemlich offenen Sitzen zur Spitze des Bauwerks hochgezogen. Dies ging ganz langsam vonstatten, aber trotzdem schauderte es Tobias: Dieser Turm war so hoch, dass er die Menschen dort oben kaum erkennen konnte. Nur ihre Beine konnte er sehen, die aus den Sitzen nach unten baumelten. Genau in diesem Moment war der höchste Punkt des Turmes erreicht. Die Anlage stoppte für eine Sekunde, dann jagten die Sitze in freiem Fall an der Außenwand des Turmes herunter. Erst kurz vor dem Boden wurden sie wieder gebremst. Tobias schauderte.

«We're going on *that* thing?» he asked Britney.

«Yeah, don't worry. It's totally cool, I promise.» Britney wasn't scared at all. That made Tobias feel a lot better. «And what is that trick you wanted to show me?» he asked.

«The penny trick! I'll show you when we're on the ride. You have to be careful, because we're not allowed to do it.» She was almost whispering the last part of what she said.

«Then it sounds good to me,» Tobias said, excited.

They arrived at the line for *The Drop*, which was a bit shorter than the one for the waterfall. They talked while they waited in line, but they kept quiet about the penny trick. They watched as people started to scream and laugh as they went up; they saw the seats reach the top, fall, and slowly brake about three-quarters of the way down. Lots of people screamed, but everyone was safe. Tobias saw that everyone was smiling as they climbed out of their seats at the bottom. Now it was their turn.

«You're up! Let's go!» shouted a tall, enthusiastic man in a park uniform and sunglasses. He let Britney, Tobias and the next fourteen people in. «Take whatever seat you like!»

Britney ran around to the far side of the tower and took a seat. Tobias followed and sat down on her left.

Sie schnallten sich fest und Britney schenkte Tobias einen Seitenblick, der zu sagen schien: «Jetzt kein Wort über den Penny-Trick!»

Tobias wollte unbedingt wissen, was es mit diesem Trick auf sich hatte. Doch noch mehr beschäftigte ihn der Gedanke, dass er gleich über 100 Meter in die Tiefe stürzen würde. Dagegen war die Wildwasserbahn vorhin der reinste Kinderkram ...

«Tobias!» he heard Britney whisper from his right. He looked and saw she was holding out a penny. They were halfway up the tower. «Put it on your knee and watch it when we fall. It'll float in the air above your knee like an UFO. It's a great trick.»

Tobias versuchte, die Münze aus Britneys Hand zu nehmen, doch der Sicherheitsgurt saß so fest, dass er nicht einmal in die Nähe von Britneys Hand kam. Britney aber schaffte es irgendwie, an Tobias' Bein heranzureichen. Vorsichtig legte sie den Penny auf seinen Oberschenkel.

«Oh, the penny trick! I forgot about that one!» said a woman on Tobias' other side. He turned around, and he saw the woman look over and laugh. They were almost on top of the tower now. Tobias looked at her. He was worried – half because he hadn't quite understood what she had said, and half because she sounded like she had noticed Britney's top-secret penny trick.

«Don't worry, honey,» the woman said in a lower voice, «I won't tell.»

Tobias understood that perfectly. He smiled back at her and said: «Thank you.»

«No problem, honey,» she replied.

Tobias schaute wieder zurück zu Britney, die den Wortwechsel zwischen ihm und der Frau offensichtlich sehr lustig fand. Zumindest grinste sie ihn breit an. Tobias grinste verschwörerisch zurück. In dieser Sekunde hatten sie den höchsten Punkt des Turmes erreicht. Tobias krallte sich an seinen Armlehnen fest, und schon ging es abwärts! Wieder fühlte Tobias sich schwerelos, doch diesmal hielt das Gefühl an, während sie scheinbar ungebremst auf den Boden zurasten. Tobias, Britney und alle anderen kreischten und johlten aus Leibeskräften. Fast hätte Tobias darüber den Penny vergessen, doch dann schaute er nach unten, und tatsächlich: die Münze schwebte, wie ein UFO, ein paar Millimeter über seinem Bein. Tobias war begeistert. Dann jedoch wurde die Münze von einem Windstoß erfasst und verschwand, auch wie ein UFO, aus seinem Blickfeld, bevor er nach ihr greifen konnte.

Tobias konnte fühlen, wie sich ihr Fall jetzt verlangsamte. Gut gebremst legten sie die letzten Meter bis zum Boden zurück. Die Sicherungsgurte öffneten sich, und gerade wollten Britney und Tobias aus ihren Sitzen steigen, da raste Tobias' UFO-Penny wieder vor ihnen durch die Luft und knallte nur ein paar Schritte vor Britney auf den Boden. Das war knapp!

This time, Britney's face exploded into laughter, and Tobias' couldn't help but laugh with her. They climbed out of their seats and onto the ground, and Britney grabbed Tobias' hand as soon as he was standing up.

«Let's go!» she said, giggling. «Let's get out of here.»

Britney pulled him by his hand as she walked as quickly as she could to the exit. As soon as they were back on the park's *Main Street*, Britney let go of his hand. She was laughing again now that they had safely escaped into the crowds of people. Both of their hearts were pounding in their chests, and Tobias couldn't stop laughing either.

«Wow! I was worried that man was going to yell at us,» Britney said.

«Me too,» nodded Tobias. Then he asked: «So, what should we do now?»

«Well, we could buy some expensive food!» Britney suggested with a smile.

«That sounds good,» Tobias agreed. «I still have twenty-five dollars. Do you think that's enough for a hamburger?» he joked.

Britney laughed. «Yeah, maybe. But you never know at this place!»

They walked until they found a restaurant called *The Frontier*. Here, too, the waiters and waitresses wore cowboy outfits. There were also TV screens in each corner playing cartoons.

They each ordered a hamburger for $ 8.50 a piece. Tobias couldn't believe how expensive it was, but at least it tasted really good.

After lunch they decided to just wander around the park, from one ride to the next.

After they had tried out the rollercoaster, they saw Madison, Björn and Anna again. Madison ran up to Britney and, half-joking, whispered: «Help! I need to speak English with someone! Björn and Anna are speaking so much German today! Please don't leave me again!»

So they spent the rest of the day at the park as a group of five. Tobias and Britney did manage to sit next to each other on every ride, but all they really wanted was to go back to *The Drop* and do the penny trick again.

Als sie am Abend wieder in Appleton ankamen, wartete Mr Summerfield schon vor der Schule auf sie. «Did you have a good time?», fragte er seine Tochter und Tobias zur Begrüßung.

«Absolutely!», antwortete Britney.

«*Six Flags* is so much fun!», fügte Tobias hinzu.

«Which one was your favorite ride?», fragte Mr Summerfield.

«*The Drop!*», sagten Britney und Tobias wie aus der Pistole geschossen.

Mr Summerfield nickte. «That's a good one. Have you two heard about the trick with the penny that floats above your leg? It's not allowed, but I heard it really works.»

Britney zwinkerte Tobias verschwörerisch zu. «I don't know, Dad», sagte sie scheinheilig, «What *is* the penny trick?»

Tobias grinste in sich hinein. Jetzt hatten Britney und er schon zwei Geheimnisse, von denen Mr Summerfield nichts zu erfahren brauchte.

Chapter Nineteen –
Das Fußballturnier ✈

Nach einem ereignislosen Schultag am Donnerstag stand am Freitag endlich das langerwartete Fußballturnier an. Als Britney und Tobias am Nachmittag auf dem Sportplatz der Roosevelt High School ankamen, wartete Madison schon ungeduldig auf sie.

«Come quick, you guys, we need to sign up for a team!», rief sie Britney und Tobias schon von weitem zu.

Die drei gingen zu einem Tisch, der am Rand des Fußballplatzes aufgestellt war und um den sich schon eine Gruppe von Schülern versammelt hatte. Auf einem Klappstuhl hinter dem Tisch saß Frau Berger, die die Organisation des Fußballturniers übernommen hatte.

«Hallo, Frau Berger», sagte Tobias. «Wir wollen uns für eine Mannschaft anmelden.»

«Das ist ganz einfach», sagte Frau Berger lächelnd und hielt ihm einen Hut hin, in dem sich zusammengefaltete Zettel befanden. «Zieht einfach jeder ein Los, dann wisst ihr, in welcher Mannschaft ihr spielt.»

Tobias nahm einen Zettel aus dem Hut. Madison und Britney taten es ihm gleich.

«I'm on team 1,» Britney said. «How about you?»

«Team 3,» Madison said.

Tobias looked at his little piece of paper. It read TEAM 3. «I'm on your team, Madison,» he said.

«Cool!» Madison said. «Does it say anywhere when we're playing?»

Right then, Mrs Berger stood up. She spoke loudly so everybody could hear her. «Here are the rules. There are six players on each team. Every match is twenty-five minutes long. Team 1 and 2 are playing in five minutes, Team 3 and 4 are playing at four o'clock. The winners of these games will play against each other at five-thirty.»

«I'm playing in five minutes,» Britney said to her friends. «I'd better go and find my team!»

«Alright,» Madison said. «We'll be cheering for you!»

«Good luck, Britney,» Tobias said.

«Thanks,» she said and gave him a big smile. How could she ever think that Tobias was an idiot? He was really sweet!

Das Spiel wurde pünktlich angepfiffen. Britney hatte sich mit ihrer Mannschaft abgesprochen und spielte wie immer als Stürmerin. Tobias staunte nicht schlecht.

Auf dem Platz standen acht Jungen und vier Mädchen, darunter ein paar richtig gute Spieler: Christoph aus Deutschland, zum Beispiel, und ein Mädchen, das Madison ihm als Janie vorgestellt hatte. Aber niemand war so schnell wie Britney. Geschickt nutzte sie jede Chance, den Ball in den gegnerischen Torraum zu bringen, und ließ dem Torwart der anderen nicht die kleinste Verschnaufpause. Nach zehn Minuten stand es bereits 2:0 – beide Tore erzielt von Britney.

«You go, girl!», hörte Tobias Madison brüllen.

«Britney vor, noch ein Tor!», rief ein deutscher Fanchor hinter ihm, und Tobias fiel begeistert mit ein.

Madison lehnte sich zu ihm hinüber und zwinkerte ihm zu. «So … what did Britney tell me you said? Girls can't play soccer?», stichelte sie.

Tobias wurde knallrot. «I … I was joking», rechtfertigte er sich.

Madison grinste nur.

Nach genau fünfundzwanzig Minuten war das Spiel vorüber. Der Endstand war 3:1 – Britney hatte in der siebzehnten Minute noch einmal getroffen, und Christoph hatte kurz vor dem Abpfiff noch den Ehrentreffer für die andere Mannschaft erzielt. «Team 1 ist im Finale, Team 2 ist leider ausgeschieden», rief Frau Berger.

Jetzt war das Match zwischen Tobias' und Madisons Mannschaft und Team 4 an der Reihe. In dieser Partie standen genau sechs Mädchen und sechs Jungen auf dem Platz. In Tobias' Mannschaft war außer ihm allerdings nur ein anderer Junge, Björn aus seiner Parallelklasse. Das kam Tobias schon etwas komisch vor. Sobald das Spiel begann, merkte er, dass dieser Umstand nur von Vorteil war: Die Mädchen stammten alle aus Britneys und Madisons Schulteam und wussten auf dem Spielfeld bestens Bescheid. Schnell stand es 1:0 – Madison und Tobias hatten dieses Tor durch einen geschickten Pass mit vorbereitet.

The audience cheered for Team 3.

«Mad' and To', go, go, go!» Britney shouted as loud as she could.

The game went on for a long time without any goals, then Team 4 scored.

«Eins zu eins – one to one,» Mrs Berger shouted.

Jetzt mussten sie sich ins Zeug legen, um das Spiel noch zu gewinnen. Tobias kickte den Ball zu Peyton, einem Mädchen aus seiner Mannschaft. Die gab den Ball ab an Björn, der ging mutig nach vorne, wich gekonnt einem Spieler des anderen Teams aus und passte dann auf Madison. Die nahm den Ball an und schoss, ohne zu zögern, aufs Tor der Gegner. Der Torwart warf sich in Richtung Ball, er berührte ihn mit den Fingerspitzen, bekam ihn jedoch nicht zu fassen: Der Ball prallte an den Innenpfosten und sprang von dort ins Netz.

«Great goal, Madison!» Tobias yelled.

«Good job!» Britney shouted.

Madison was giving high-fives to everyone on the team.

«Two to one for Team 3!» Mrs Berger announced.

There were only two more minutes left. Team 4 had one more chance to score, but this time, the goalie caught the ball as he dived for it.

Then, time ran out and the whistle blew.

«Team 3 wins! Team 1 and team 3 are in the final!» Mrs Berger shouted. Her voice was hoarse from all the shouting, but she seemed to be having just as much fun as the students.

«Congratulations you two!» Britney said when Madison and Tobias walked off the field. She first hugged her best friend, and then she hugged Tobias. He had felt great before, but getting a hug from Britney made him feel even better.

«Thanks. But you know that we'll have to beat *your* team next!» Madison joked.

«We'll see about that!» Britney grinned.

Um genau fünf Uhr dreißig marschierten Team 1 und Team 3 aufs Feld. Es hatten sich jetzt viel mehr Zuschauer am Spielfeldrand versammelt, die lautstark beide Mannschaften anfeuerten.

Der Pfiff zum Spielbeginn erklang. Sofort erkämpfte Britneys Team sich den Ball, doch Björn und Peyton gewannen ihn in einer taktisch klugen Aktion zurück. Das Publikum applaudierte.

Eine Weile ging der Ball zwischen Spielern des Team 3 hin und her, doch dann kam Britneys Team wieder zum Zug. Als der Ball sich dem gegnerischen Torraum näherte, war Britney wieder in ihrem Element: Elegant nahm sie den Pass ihres Mitspielers an und kickte den Ball mit voller Wucht ins Tor. Für den Torwart gab es nichts zu halten: Er konnte dem Ball nur noch hinterhergucken.

Jetzt jubelte das Publikum für Team 1.

«Britney, Britney,» the audience shouted.

«One to nothing for Team 1!» Mrs Berger announced.

Madison and Tobias weren't so happy for Britney this time.

«Damn it!» Madison muttered to herself. Then she turned to Tobias and shouted: «Come on, Tobias, let's do it! We can still beat them!»

Tobias knew he was going to have to give his absolute best to help his team win the game now.

Gleich nach dem eins zu null hatte Britney noch zwei weitere Torchancen. Beide Male prallte der Ball jedoch am Pfosten ab. Jetzt war endlich wieder Team 3 am Zug. Madison passte auf Peyton, die ging nach vorn und gab den Ball an Björn weiter. Jetzt stand Tobias günstig zum Schuss. «Hierher!», rief er, und

Björn reagierte sofort mit einer hohen Flanke in die Richtung, aus der Tobias gerufen hatte. Tobias sprang in die Fluglinie des Balls, köpfte und … TOR!

«Na also!», dachte Tobias.

«Eins zu eins! One to one!» Mrs Berger shouted excitedly.

Madison and her other teammates cheered for him.

The people in the audience were all screaming and clapping for him, too.

«Great job, Tobias!»

«Go, Team 3!»

«Olé, olé, olé, olé», hörte Tobias die Zuschauer rufen. Jetzt fühlte er sich richtig siegessicher. Allerdings lagen noch zehn Spielminuten vor ihnen – zehn Minuten, in denen sich entscheiden würde, wer das Turnier gewinnt.

Die Spielerinnen und Spieler auf dem Platz gaben noch einmal ihr Bestes. Beide Mannschaften griffen mutig an, passten sich den Ball geschickt zu und erspielten mehrere Torchancen. Als Björn eine besonders brenzlige Situation im eigenen Torraum zu klären versuchte, passierte es: Sein Fuß verfehlte den Ball um einige Zentimeter. Björn verlor dadurch das Gleichgewicht, krachte mit voller Wucht gegen den Torpfosten und blieb benommen auf dem Rasen liegen.

«Time out! Injury!» the referee called.

All the players gathered around Björn. He was sitting on the ground now, holding his head.

«Are you o.k.?», «Does your head hurt?» everybody asked.

After only a little while, Björn slowly got up. «I think I'm o.k. again. Really, I'm fine.»

Everybody was relieved. The accident had looked worse than it really was.

Der Schiedsrichter pfiff das Match wieder an. Nur noch drei Minuten, dann war die Spielzeit vorbei, und immer noch stand es eins zu eins. Noch zwei Minuten. Noch eine. Plötzlich jedoch rief der Schiedsrichter: «Five minutes extra time!»

«Fünf Minuten Nachspielzeit wegen der Unterbrechung», übersetzte Frau Berger.

Den Spielerinnen und Spielern war die Anstrengung jetzt anzumerken. Weite Pässe im Mittelfeld bestimmten die letzten Minuten. Manche Zuschauer pfiffen, andere spornten die Teams durch Zurufe an. Keiner auf dem Platz schien noch in bester Form. Doch dann, eine Minute vor dem endgültigen Abpfiff, kam die entscheidende Wendung: Peyton verlor den Ball, den Tobias ihr zugespielt hatte, an ein Mädchen des anderen Teams. Diese flankte auf einen Mitspieler, der den Ball in Richtung des gegnerischen Tores schoss. Britney stürmte auf den Ball zu, nahm ihn noch in der Luft an, machte eine akrobatische Drehung und – Tobias hielt den Atem an – beförderte das Leder mit einem Fallrückzieher ins Netz. In der gleichen Sekunde ertönte der Schlusspfiff.

Die Zuschauer tobten. Solch ein Tor hatten die meisten von ihnen bisher nur im Fernsehen gesehen.

«Tor! Tor!», rief Frau Berger. «Team 1 hat das Turnier gewonnen!»

Everybody was cheering for Britney again, and her team was carrying her around the field. Britney was the star of the tournament!

Nach dem letzten Spiel begannen die Vorbereitungen für das Barbecue. Es gab einen riesigen Grill, auf dem Steaks, Würstchen und Hamburger gebraten wurden. Es roch schon richtig gut, und Tobias merkte, wie hungrig ihn das Fußballspielen gemacht hatte.

Ein bisschen ärgerte er sich, dass seine Mannschaft das Endspiel verloren hatte, aber eins musste er zugeben: Britney war wirklich eine gute Fußballspielerin, und ihr Team hatte verdient gewonnen. Ein Grund mehr, sich endlich für seine blöde Bemerkung von vor zwei Wochen zu entschuldigen. Er entdeckte Britney am Spielfeldrand und ging zu ihr hinüber.

«Hey,» she said when she saw him. «Good game!»

«Thank you,» Tobias answered. «Good game, too!»

Britney smiled.

«Your last goal was great!» Tobias continued.

«You liked my bicycle kick?» she said proudly.

«Bicycle kick?» Tobias asked. Then he realized what she meant. «Oh, that kick is called ‹Fallrückzieher› in German.»

«Fall… what?» Britney asked. She tried to say the word a few times, but she couldn't quite get it right. «German is so hard …!» she complained, but she was still smiling. Tobias smiled back at her.

«Jetzt oder nie», dachte er.

«Ääh …» he began, «there is something I wanted to say.»

Britney gave him a surprised look.

Tobias was really embarrassed now, and it was hard to find the right words. «I wanted to say that … two weeks ago … I'm sorry that I said that girls shouldn't play soccer.»

Britney wanted to say something, but Tobias continued: «It was a joke. I'm sorry I made you angry.»

Then it was Britney's turn to look a little embarrassed. «I'm sorry I got so angry. How do you say this in German? Es tut … Es tut mir Leid!»

«Mir tut es auch Leid», Tobias said.

«But we're friends now, right?» Britney said and playfully punched him in the side.

Tobias nodded and smiled. He felt so much better than before.

«Why don't we go and get something to eat? I would love some bratwurst – how about you?» Britney asked.

«I'm really hungry, too!» Tobias agreed.

Britney took his arm in hers. «Let's go eat!» she said.

Kapitel Zwanzig –
Finally Spring Break ✈

Nach den aufregenden Ereignissen der Woche verbrachten Tobias und Britney zwei ruhige Tage im Hause Summerfield. Sie schliefen morgens lange, guckten DVDs, spielten Videospiele und ließen sich von Mr und Mrs Summerfield bekochen. Am Sonntagabend saßen Tobias und Britney mit Britneys Eltern in der Küche und berieten, wie die letzte Woche von Tobias' Aufenthalt verbracht werden könnte. Roosevelt High School und der Kindergarten von Britneys Schwester Brianne waren für die Frühlingsferien geschlossen, die Eltern hatten sich freigenommen – einem Kurzurlaub stand nichts im Weg.

«So where would you like to go?», fragte Mr Summerfield Tobias.

«Mmmh, I don't know.» Tobias musste über diese Frage erst mal nachdenken. Dann hatte er eine Idee: «To the beach in California!»

Mr Summerfield lachte. «That's maybe a *little* too far away. It's a good five-day drive from here to California!»

«Oh», sagte Tobias. Er hatte ganz vergessen, wie riesig die USA waren.

«If you would like to see some water, we could drive up North to Brown Bear Lake!», bot Mrs Summerfield an.

«My parents have a little cottage there», erklärte Britney. «It's right by the water, and there's a little beach, too. It's really nice.»

«That sounds great!», sagte Tobias. Ob sie nun ans Meer

oder an einen See fuhren, solange es Wasser gab, war Tobias zufrieden.

On Monday morning, the Summerfield family and Tobias were on their way to Northern Wisconsin. This time, they rode in the Ford Excursion. Tobias still couldn't believe how big the car was. It easily seated five people, and there were also bags, backpacks, and boxes of food for the whole week. Mr and Mrs Summerfield were sitting in the front, Tobias and Britney were sitting in the middle, and Brianne was sitting in the back.

The little girl was wearing headphones and staring at a monitor in front of her, happily singing along with the music. Tobias saw that she was watching Sesame Street. Elmo was singing a song with some big furry monster.

«We always bring a DVD for Brianne,» Mr Summerfield explained.

«That makes the drive a lot more enjoyable for everybody,» Mrs Summerfield smiled.

Tobias war beeindruckt. «Das ist ja wie im Flugzeug!», dachte er.

Nach vier Stunden Fahrt durch eine Landschaft, die hauptsächlich aus Feldern, Weiden und Wäldern bestand, waren sie am Ziel. Mrs Summerfield parkte den Ford neben einem rustikalen Holzhaus, und alle sprangen aus dem Wagen.

«Come on, Tobias, I'll show you the lake!», rief Britney. Die beiden liefen um das Haus herum und durch ein kleines Waldstück. Und da lag er vor ihnen: Brown Bear Lake, ein riesiger See, dessen Ufer gesäumt war von dunklen Tannen und einigen versprengten Blockhäusern.

«Isn't it pretty?» Britney asked.

Tobias nodded. It was very pretty. Unfortunately, it was also very cold, much colder than in Appleton. Tobias wished he had packed a warmer jacket. Britney was only wearing a sweater and she looked cold, too. «Come inside, you two!» they heard Mrs Summerfield's voice through the woods. «Dad is making hot chocolate for everybody!»

«Yummie,» Britney said. «I love hot chocolate.»

«What is yummie?» Tobias asked.

«That's something you say when you really like the way something tastes,» Britney explained.

«Oh!» Tobias said. «Lecker!»

«An *easy* German word!» Britney said jokingly, «I *can't* believe it!»

Tobias laughed.

«Brit! Tobias!» they heard Mrs Summerfield call again.

«We're coming, Mom!» Britney shouted. Then the two turned around and sprinted back to the cottage.

When they arrived in the kitchen, there were two steaming cups of hot chocolate waiting for them.

«Would you like some marshmallows in your hot chocolate?» Britney asked.

Tobias wasn't so sure.

Britney noticed his doubtful look.

«You should try it! It tastes great!» she told him.

Tobias decided to give it a try. Like Britney, he put some marshmallows in his hot chocolate and stirred. Then he took a sip: it was *very* sweet, and *very* good.

«Do you like it?» Britney asked.

«Yes,» Tobias said.

«I think it's the *best*!» Britney said.

Mr Summerfield entered the kitchen. «How's the hot chocolate, you two?»

«Lecker!» yelled Britney.

«Yummie!» Tobias shouted. Mr Summerfield smiled. «Seems like drinking hot chocolate isn't only a great way to stay warm. It's also a great way to learn a new language!» he thought to himself.

Chapter Twenty-one – *Deutsche Wurzeln* ✈

Nachdem sie sich etwas aufgewärmt hatten, schlossen sich Britney und Tobias dem Rest der Familie zu einem Spaziergang am Brown Bear Lake an. Sie gingen auf einem breiten Streifen aus Sand und Steinen am Ufer, der hin und wieder durch eine Baumgruppe unterbrochen wurde. Brianne patschte in ihren Gummistiefeln durch das seichte Wasser.

«So, what do you think about Brown Bear Lake, Tobias? It's a lot different than Appleton, huh?», fragte Mr Summerfield.

Tobias nickte. «It is very nice here», antwortete er.

«There are six more lakes in the area, and huge forests. And, of course, there is a lot of flat land», erklärte Mrs Summerfield.

Die Landschaft hatte Tobias sich schon auf der Autofahrt angeguckt. Sie erinnerte ihn an Fotos, die seine Eltern von einem Skandinavienurlaub mitgebracht hatten. Deshalb sagte er: «It looks a little bit like Scandinavia.»

Mr und Mrs Summerfield schien das nicht zu überraschen. «As a matter of fact, many families in Wisconsin are originally from Scandinavia», erzählte Mr Summerfield. «Their great-grandparents came to America, and they stayed in Wisconsin because it reminded them of their home.»

Tobias nickte interessiert. Das hatte er gar nicht gewusst. Ob die Vorfahren der Summerfields wohl auch aus Skandinavien stammten?

«Is your family from Scandinavia, too?», fragte er.

Mrs Summerfield nickte. «I'm Norwegian and Swedish», erklärte sie. «Before I married Britney's father, my last name was Svenson.»

Der Name klang auch in Tobias' Ohren sehr skandinavisch. Aber woher kam wohl der Name Summerfield? Tobias tippte auf England.

«Where is your family from, Mr Summerfield?», fragte er Britneys Vater.

Mr Summerfield grinste ihn an. «I'm all German!», sagte er.

Tobias war überrascht. «Summerfield» konnte doch nie im Leben ein deutscher Name sein! Britney sah die Überraschung auf Tobias' Gesicht.

«When my great-great-grandfather came to America, his name was Sommerfeld. They changed it to Summerfield because it sounds more like English», klärte sie ihn auf.

«Ach so!», dachte Tobias. Das machte natürlich Sinn.

«There are a lot more names like that», fügte Mr Summerfield hinzu. «Do you know Chrysler? They make cars here in America. When they first came from Germany generations ago, their name was Kreisler. Or the famous Rockefeller family? They used to be farmers in Germany, and their name was Roggenfelder.»

«Wow!», sagte Tobias. Er war wirklich beeindruckt von diesen neuen Informationen.

Gerade wollte er noch eine Frage stellen, da wechselte Mrs Summerfield schon das Thema.

«Do you know what you would like to do tomorrow?», fragte sie ihre Tochter und Tobias.

«I thought that we could get the boat out tomorrow. Or we could go on a hike and have picnic somewhere», schlug Britney vor. Dann wandte sie sich an Tobias. «How about you? Do you like canoes, or would you like to go hiking?»

Da Tobias sich besonders auf den Urlaub am Wasser gefreut hatte, fiel ihm die Antwort leicht. «Let's get the canoe out!», sagte er.

Kapitel Zweiundzwanzig –
That's Some Bad Weather out There! ✈

The next morning, Britney was woken up by a loud drumming sound. She opened her eyes and looked to the window. Normally, she could see the lake from here. But today things were different. Instead of the calm blue lake and some tall green trees Britney saw only one thing: rain. It was raining so hard that all there seemed to be outside was water. Britney sighed and pulled the blanket over her head. There was no chance of a canoe tour in this weather.

Everybody got up late that day. After a long breakfast, it was still raining. Although it was hardly possible, it seemed like the rain was getting even harder.

Mr Summerfield had switched on the weather forecast on TV. «I don't think we'll be able to leave the house any time soon,» he said. «It looks like heavy rain all day.»

«Oh man …» Britney complained. «What are we going to do?»

«I'm sure you two will find something to do around the house,» Mrs Summerfield tried to cheer Britney up. Then she gave her daughter a big smile: «And you can always play with Brianne, you know! Your father and I wouldn't mind at all if you did …»

Britney didn't like this suggestion at all. But since she had no better ideas, Tobias and Britney spent the day with Brianne, doing Brianne's favorite activities: they played with building blocks, read children's books and drew pictures. They were in the middle of a game of Memory when Mrs Summerfield told them it was time for dinner.

«You've been great babysitters!» she said to them. «As a reward, Dad and I made a nice big dinner. And for dessert, I tried a new cake recipe. How does that sound, Tobias?»

«Mmmmh, great!», sagte Tobias begeistert. Brianne war ja ganz niedlich, aber langsam hatte er genug. Das stundenlange Spielen hatte ihn richtig hungrig gemacht.

«How about you, darling, are you hungry?», fragte Mrs Summerfield ihre ältere Tochter.

«Definitely!», sagte Britney.

«No, they're not hungry!» Brianne's voice piped up. «They want to play, mom!»

Mrs Summerfield laughed. «Come here, sweetie,» she said and picked her little daughter up. «We'll have some dinner, and then the three of you can finish the game.»

Brianne protested all the way to the dining room. She didn't forget about their Memory game until she spotted the big cake that Mr Summerfield had put in the middle of the dinner table.

«Chocolate cake! Yummie!» Brianne screamed.

«‹Yummie› is ‹lecker› in German, did you know?» Britney jokingly told her sister and gave Tobias a big smile.

«Lecker! Lecker, lecker, lecker!» squeaked Brianne and everybody laughed.

Nach dem Abendessen – Tobias hatte drei Stück Torte verdrückt – übernahmen Britney und Tobias freiwillig den Abwasch. Mr und Mrs Summerfield spielten dafür das Memory-Spiel mit Brianne zu Ende, bevor sie sie ins Bett brachten.

After that, Tobias, Britney and her parents sat down in front of the TV and watched two movies: a comedy and an old Western. Everybody had a great time.

Als Mr and Mrs Summerfield um kurz vor Mitternacht beide auf dem Sofa eingeschlafen waren, beschlossen auch Tobias und Britney, ins Bett zu gehen. Um die Erwachsenen nicht zu wecken, schlichen sie auf Zehenspitzen aus dem Wohnzimmer. Vor Tobias' Schlafzimmertür blieben sie stehen.

«Goodnight, Tobias», sagte Britney und umarmte ihn.

«Gute Nacht», murmelte er und umarmte Britney zaghaft zurück. Dann schlüpfte sie aus seinen Armen, lief die Treppe zu ihrem Schlafzimmer hinauf, winkte ihm noch einmal lächelnd zu und verschwand hinter ihrer Tür. Tobias stand noch einen Moment da und schaute Britney hinterher. Dann ging er auch in sein Zimmer. Dass es draußen immer noch in Strömen regnete, hatten beide ganz vergessen.

Chapter Twenty-three

Immer mit der Ruhe ✈

Als Tobias am nächsten Morgen aufwachte, erwartete ihn ein gänzlich anderes Bild als am vorangegangenen Tag: Vor dem Fenster lag der See glasklar und still, der Himmel war wolkenlos, von Regen keine Spur. Begeistert sprang er aus dem Bett. Endlich konnten sie wieder nach draußen! Dem Bootsausflug, der gestern im wahrsten Sinne des Wortes ins Wasser gefallen war, stand nichts mehr im Wege.

So, after a quick breakfast consisting of cornflakes and O.J., Tobias and Britney were on their way to the lake. Between them, they were carrying a wooden canoe. Once they got to the shore, they dropped it down into the water.

«That boat is heavy!» Tobias said and rubbed his aching hands together.

Britney seemed a little exhausted, too, but she was too excited to pause.

«Come on, let's get going!», sagte sie und kletterte geschickt an Bord.

Tobias versuchte, es ihr nachzumachen, doch es war nicht so leicht, wie es aussah. Trotz der Windstille wackelte das Boot hin und her, und Tobias, der noch mit einem Bein auf festem Boden stand, hatte Mühe, sein Gleichgewicht zu halten. Britney kam ihm zur Hilfe. Sie streckte ihm beide Hände zum Festhalten entgegen, er griff zu, und mit einem großen Schritt war auch Tobias trockenen Fußes an Bord.

Like the night before, they stood really close to each other.

For a short moment, they didn't move at all. Then Tobias realized that he was still holding Britney's hands. He took a step back and looked at her face. Britney's face had turned a little pink, but she stood completely still. Tobias realized that he had a funny feeling in his stomach. They stayed just like that for another moment, then Britney suddenly let go of his hands.

«Maybe we should start paddling,» she said. Her voice sounded a little funny.

«O.k.», stimmte Tobias schnell zu. Er griff sich ein Ruder und reichte Britney das andere. Wortlos setzten sie sich auf die gegenüberliegenden Bänke des Kanus und begannen zu paddeln. Erst ging es nur im Kreis, doch bald hatten sie die Technik heraus und kamen gut voran. Sie paddelten schweigend vor sich hin, und nach ungefähr fünfzehn Minuten hatten sie die Mitte des Sees erreicht. Tobias schaute sich um. Das Wasser um sie herum lag glatt wie ein Spiegel, und auch die Bäume in der Ferne standen still vor dem klaren blauen Himmel, an dem die Sonne freundlich strahlte. Es herrschte absolute Ruhe: Kein Wind rauschte durch die Baumwipfel, keine Vögel zwitscherten, keine menschlichen Stimmen waren zu hören.

Keine menschlichen Stimmen? Tobias und Britney fuhren auf. Dort hinten, vor dem Haus der Summerfields, stand eine Person, die wild mit den Armen gestikulierte und etwas in ihre Richtung zu brüllen schien.

«That's my Dad!» Britney said, sounding surprised. «What is he saying?»

Tobias tried to listen hard, but he could not understand a

word. They were simply too far away. Mr Summerfield was still waving like crazy.

«I think he wants us to come back to the house,» Britney said.

«But why?» Tobias asked. The weather was so nice, why should they get off the boat?

«I have no idea,» Britney replied and looked at her father. He was still waving and shouting. «It seems to be important,» she added.

Tobias could tell that she was right. They both took up their paddles, and they rowed back to the shore as fast as they could. When they got there about ten minutes later, Mr Summerfield was already waiting for them.

«Come on, kids, we have to get back inside the house!» he shouted when they jumped off the boat. Tobias could tell that Mr Summerfield was very serious about this.

«What's going on, Dad?» Britney asked, but Mr Summerfield wasn't listening. He had already picked up the canoe, and he was carrying it back to the house, all on his own.

«Come on!» he yelled over his shoulder. All that Britney and Tobias could do was grab the paddles and follow him.

When they arrived at the cottage, Mr and Mrs Summerfield and Brianne were waiting for them in the living room.

«I'm so glad Dad found you!» Mrs Summerfield said when the two arrived.

«Could someone tell us what's going on?» Britney asked impatiently.

«We watched the weather forecast on TV,» Mr Summerfield began. «And there's a severe thunderstorm warning for Brown Bear County. There's a huge front headed right for us.»

«Oh no,» Britney sighed and plunged down on the sofa.

Tobias was very surprised. The weather was great, how could there be a storm? So he said to Mr Summerfield: «But the weather is really nice!»

«That's right,» Mr Summerfield said. «But did you notice how quiet it was? There was no sound outside at all. That is always a sign for a tornado.»

Tobias war plötzlich ganz flau zumute. Ein Tornado?! Er wusste nicht viel über Stürme, aber er erinnerte sich noch gut an den Film *Twister*, den er mal auf Video gesehen hatte: Darin war es um einen Tornado gegangen, und Tobias sah ganz deutlich eine Szene vor sich, in der Menschen, Häuser, ja sogar eine Kuh durch die Luft gewirbelt wurden.

«We will be o.k., Tobias,» Mrs Summerfield told him. «We've been through a few of these, and we're always o.k.»

«We all just have to stay inside until it's over,» Mr Summerfield added. «Just to be on the safe side.»

«And we can follow the weather forecast on TV,» Mrs Summerfield said.

«And we can all play together!» Brianne shouted excitedly.

«Great!» Britney said sarcastically. «Another day inside the house, another day playing baby games.»

«Mom!» Brianne whined. «Britney is mean to me!»

Mrs Summerfield ignored her daughters' quarrel.

«Why don't Dad and I play another game of Memory with you, Brianne?» she said to her little daughter. «And you two,» she looked at Britney and Tobias, «you should go to Britney's room. Dad and I got something out of the basement for the two of you. Why don't you go and take a look?»

Was auch immer diese Überraschung war, Tobias war für jede Ablenkung zu haben. Er folgte Britney also gespannt in ihr Zimmer. Dort angekommen, sahen sie sofort, wovon Mrs Summerfield gesprochen hatte: In der Mitte des Raumes stand ein Kickertisch. Schon etwas abgenutzt, aber offensichtlich voll funktionsfähig.

«Cool! A foosball table!» Britney shouted.

Tobias was excited, too. «Let's play!» he said. Then, instead of walking over to the table, he paused and gave Britney a surprised look. «What is this game called in English?»

«Foosball!» Britney repeated. «Sounds like the German word ‹Fußball›, huh?»

Tobias prägte sich das neue Wort gleich ein. «Soccer», «Foosball», «Football» – vor dem Austausch hätte er nicht sagen können, was diese Vokabeln genau bedeuten, jetzt schienen sie ihm sonnenklar.

«O.k., let's play!» Britney said. «You take the green team, and I'm yellow.»

So verging der Rest des Vormittags. Britney und Tobias kämpften fast so ehrgeizig wie auf dem richtigen Fußballplatz, und immer abwechselnd gewann mal das grüne und mal das gelbe Team. Sie spielten, bis Mr Summerfield sie zum Mittagessen rief.

There was only a small lunch that day: sandwiches and potato chips. Everybody ate in the living room, because that's where the only TV was. The weather forecast continued as the storm moved in.

«It looks like the storm is almost here,» Mrs Summerfield said and took a bite from her sandwich.

Her husband nodded. «Maybe another five or ten minutes before it gets here.»

Tobias schaute aus dem Fenster. Eigentlich sah es draußen noch genauso freundlich aus wie am Morgen. Nur der Himmel schien jetzt etwas verhangener, das Sonnenlicht etwas trüber.

«I guess we will have to go to the basement pretty soon,» Mr Summerfield said.

Tobias fühlte wieder dieses flaue Gefühl in der Magengrube. Einerseits sagten alle, es würde nicht so schlimm werden, und dann mussten sie trotzdem in den Keller? In seinen Ohren klang das *ziemlich* gefährlich.

Britney and Brianne didn't like the idea either.

«It's so boring in the basement, Dad!» Britney complained.

«I always get scared down there!» Brianne whined.

«Don't worry, you two,» Mrs Summerfield said. «We'll take the radio and some games, and we also have some of the chocolate cake left! You won't even notice that we're in the basement.»

This was enough to convince Brianne, but Britney still looked unhappy. Then Tobias had an idea.

«Can we bring the foosball table to the basement?» he asked.

«That's a great idea!» Britney's face brightened up immediately. «Can we, Mom?»

«Sure! That is a good idea, Tobias,» Mrs Summerfield agreed.

Mr Summerfield, who had just finished his sandwich, got up. «Why don't I bring the foosball table downstairs,» he said and looked at his wife, «and you bring the radio and some food.»

Mrs Summerfield nodded.

«And I'll bring some games!» Brianne shouted.

«Alright,» Mr Summerfield agreed. «Finish your lunch, and then I'll see everybody downstairs in a minute.»

Kapitel Vierundzwanzig – *Tornado!* ✈

Der Keller des Blockhauses war gemütlicher, als Tobias gedacht hatte. There was only one small window, but, other than that, the basement looked like an ordinary living room. There was a couch, some comfortable chairs and a little table on which Mrs Summerfield had put the cake, drinks and some snacks. Brianne had scattered her toys and games all over the floor. Mr Summerfield was sitting on the couch with a small radio on his lap. He was listening to the weather forecast again. Mrs

Summerfield and Brianne were sitting in one of the chairs and looking at a photo album. The foosball table was in the middle of the room now, and Britney and Tobias started playing again.

«… green midfield passes the ball to forward, forward aims, shoots … green team scores!» Britney shouted. «One to nothing for me!»

Tobias laughed. «You're not only a good player, you're also a good commentator!» he said to her.

And then, all of a sudden, Tobias forgot all about the foosball table, or Britney, or anything else that had just been on his mind.

«BOOM!!»

Ein Donnerschlag erschütterte das Blockhaus – so stark, dass die Wände wie bei einem Erdstoß vibrierten. Tobias zuckte zusammen. Britney ließ vor Schreck den kleinen Kickerball fallen. Brianne schrie erschreckt auf und vergrub ihr Gesicht in den Armen ihrer Mutter.

No one spoke. The thunder had gone, but it was still loud outside. Heavy rain was hitting hard against the small window now, and the wind was noisily blowing through the forest. Tobias could see lightning, and then there was another roar of thunder.

«BOOM!!»

Tobias war sich sicher, dass er noch niemals zuvor ein solches Unwetter erlebt hatte. Das laute Krachen des Donners hatte ihm einen Schrecken eingejagt, doch der herunterprasselnde Regen beunruhigte ihn noch mehr. Würde der See den

Regen aufnehmen können, oder stand eine große Überflutung bevor? Womöglich war der Weg zurück nach Appleton durch das Unwetter abgeschnitten, und sie saßen im Ferienhaus fest! Und was, wenn es durch den Blitzschlag zu einem Feuer kommen würde? Und was würde erst passieren, wenn der Tornado diese Gegend erreichte?

«Mom! I'm scared!» Brianne broke the silence.

Mrs Summerfield held her daughter in her arms and stroke her hair. «We'll be alright, kids. Don't worry,» Mrs Summerfield said. She had to speak much louder than usual because of the drumming rain. «This storm is nothing to be scared about.»

Then, another crash of thunder.

«BOOM!!»

It made the house shake again, as if nature was making fun of Mrs Summerfield's words.

«Really, this thunderstorm is a good thing,» Mrs Summerfield said. «Once this thunderstorm passes through, we know the tornado will have missed us,» she explained.

«That's true.» Mr Summerfield nodded. «This storm seems a little scary, but we're safe in here.»

Tobias wusste nicht, ob er das glauben sollte. Er hörte das tobende Unwetter, durch das schmale Kellerfenster sah er immer wieder grelle Blitze aufleuchten. Er fühlte sich überhaupt nicht sicher! Andererseits hatten die Summerfields sicher schon mehrere Stürme erlebt, sie wussten bestimmt, wovon sie sprachen. Oder wollten sie ihre Kinder nur in Sicherheit wiegen?

Britney had been quiet for a while. She had sat down on the couch and tried to listen to the radio.

«Turn up the radio, dad. Let's hear what they're saying,» she suggested.

Mr Summerfield turned up the volume. Now everybody could here the newsreaders' voice: «... heavy thunderstorms and strong winds in Northern Wisconsin, especially in the Brown Bear Lake Area. Several roads are blocked due to fallen trees. The tornado itself has moved into Chippewa county ...»

«Thank God!» Britney sighed. «Mom was right: the tornado is gone!»

Auch Tobias fühlte sich durch diese Nachricht etwas beruhigter. Die im Radio wussten sicherlich am besten, wie die Wetterlage war.

«Do you want to play some more foosball?», fragte er Britney. «Sure,» she said and walked over to the table. «What was the score? Oh yeah, one to nothing for me.»

Sie hatten gerade fünf Minuten gespielt, und Tobias lag – sehr zu Britneys Ärger – mit zwei zu eins in Führung, als ein weiterer Donnerschlag das Blockhaus erschütterte. Er schien noch lauter und bedrohlicher als zuvor. Und dann geschah es: Das Licht im Keller flackerte kurz und erstarb. Brianne kreischte. Mr Summerfield fluchte. Britney und Tobias brachten vor Schreck kein Wort heraus. Es war stockdunkel. Nur durch die Blitze wurde der Raum hin und wieder etwas erhellt.

Brianne was crying silently in her mother's arms. Britney

and Tobias slowly walked over to the couch and sat down with everybody else. There was no way they could play foosball now. At least they could still listen to the radio, it was running on batteries.

Langsam gewöhnten sich Tobias' Augen ein bisschen an die Dunkelheit. Er sah, wie Mr Summerfield, der kurz den Keller verlassen hatte, um nach dem Grund für den Stromausfall zu suchen, wieder durch die Tür trat.

«Everything is fine upstairs. But I have no idea what caused the electricity to go out,» he said to everyone.

«What are we going to do now, Dad?» Britney asked.

«I guess all we can do is wait,» Mr Summerfield answered.

«Nooooo, I don't want to wait!» Brianne whined.

Durch die Dunkelheit erschien der Sturm, der draußen tobte, noch gefährlicher. Tobias gruselte sich selbst ein bisschen, und Brianne tat ihm richtig Leid. «Kein Wunder, dass die Kleine solche Angst hat!», dachte er bei sich.

«Why don't we all play a game?» Mrs Summerfield suggested to her younger daughter. «Some games are extra-fun when they are played in the dark!»

«Noooooo!» Brianne whined.

«Maybe we can listen to some nice music on the radio!» Mr Summerfield suggested. But that idea didn't cheer Brianne up either.

«Nooooo!» she cried.

Now Britney tried to make her sister feel better.

«I can tell you a story if you want!» she said to Brianne.

«Noooooo!» Brianne screamed.

Tobias erinnerte Briannes Verhalten an ihr Gequengel vom vergangenen Abend, als sie nicht einsehen wollte, dass es Zeit zum Abendessen war. Dieser Gedanke brachte ihn plötzlich auf eine Idee.

«Hey Brianne!» Tobias said to the little girl. «How about a CHOCOLATE CAKE PICNIC?»

To everybody's surprise – especially Tobias' – Brianne stopped crying. Although it was dark, Tobias could tell that she was staring at him. «What is a chocolate cake picnic?» she said in a voice that still sounded a little whiny.

So Tobias needed to use his imagination. «We all take a pillow,» he said, «and we sit down on it on the floor.»

Brianne was still looking at him expectantly.

«And then we all take something to drink,» Tobias continued, «and a BIG piece of chocolate cake.»

Brianne was nodding excitedly.

«And that's called a chocolate cake picnic,» Tobias finished.

Brianne smiled and jumped up. «Mom! Dad! Britney! Let's have a chocolate cake picnic!» she shouted excitedly.

Alle machten mit, und ein paar Minuten später saßen die Summerfields und Tobias im Kreis auf dem Fußboden und aßen Schokoladentorte. Brianne strahlte. Gewitter und Dunkelheit schien sie ganz vergessen zu haben.

«Great job, Tobias!» Mr Summerfield said. «I thought we'd never calm her down.»

«That was a wonderful idea!» Britney whispered into his ear and secretly squeezed his hand in the dark.

Jetzt strahlte auch Tobias.

Gerade als Brianne sich den letzten Krümel Torte in den Mund geschoben hatte, flackerte plötzlich das Licht an der Decke des Kellers. Erst nur ganz schwach, doch dann strahlte die Lampe, als wäre sie nie ausgefallen.

«Yippee!» Brianne screamed and started dancing around the room.

Britney and Tobias had jumped up, too.

«Finally!» Britney shouted.

«Listen everybody,» Mr Summerfield said. «The storm is moving away, too!»

Tobias listened. Mr Summerfield was right. It was still raining hard, but the loud thunder had gone away.

«I think it's safe to go upstairs now,» Mrs Summerfield said.

Britney and Tobias looked at each other. Then they ran out of the room and up the stairs. The storm was finally over! And it felt *so good* to be out of the basement again!

Chapter Twenty-five –
Endspurt ✈

Nach dem aufregenden Tag mit Tornado-Alarm verlief der Rest der Woche am Brown Bear Lake sehr geruhsam. Tobias und Britney machten Wanderungen, paddelten noch ein paarmal auf dem See und machten es sich am Abend mit Mr Summerfields heißer Schokolade gemütlich. Obwohl nichts Außergewöhnliches vorfiel, vergingen die Tage wie im Flug. Als der Samstag gekommen war und die Summerfields das Auto für die Rückfahrt nach Hause packten, wurde Tobias zum ersten Mal bewusst, dass die drei Wochen des Austausches schon fast vorüber waren: Schon in weniger als 24 Stunden ging es wieder nach Deutschland.

Aus diesem Grund schaute Tobias auch etwas wehmütig auf den Brown Bear Lake und das Blockhaus zurück, als der Ford Excursion sich in Richtung Appleton in Bewegung setzte. Auch Britney war stiller als sonst, als sie neben ihm im Auto saß und die Landschaft an ihnen vorüberzog.

Back in Appleton, there was not much time for anything. Tobias had to pack the rest of his belongings, and the Summerfield family was busy unloading bags and backpacks and doing a lot of laundry. It was only after dinner that Tobias and Britney got to spend some time together on their own. They were sitting outside on the door steps of the Summerfield house, both looking pretty unhappy.

«I can't believe you're going home tomorrow!» Britney said.

Tobias nodded. «I don't want to go home,» he said.

They were silent for a while.

Then Britney asked: «Do you want to know something?»

«What?» Tobias asked.

«Do you remember when you first found out that you were going to stay with me?» she asked.

«Of course,» Tobias answered. «Why?»

«Because I just remembered that I was really angry when I found out that you were coming,» Britney told him and smiled. «I really wanted a girl, not a boy.»

Tobias laughed. «I was angry, too. I shouted at Mrs Berger when I found out that I had to stay with you,» Tobias confessed.

Now Britney laughed. Then she asked: «Are you still angry about that?»

Tobias could feel his cheeks turn pink. «No,» he said. «I'm glad that I stayed with you.»

«Me, too,» Britney said.

They didn't say anything for a while.

«You know what's a good thing?» Britney asked.

«What?» Tobias asked back.

«That I'll be coming to Germany in the summer,» Britney said.

Daran hatte Tobias auch schon gedacht. Im Sommer kamen die amerikanischen Schüler zum Gegenbesuch nach Deutschland. Das hieß, dass er Britney schon in ein paar Monaten wiedersehen würde.

«That *is* a good thing», stimmte Tobias ihr zu.

Sie saßen eine Weile schweigend da. Dann beschloss Tobias, etwas zu tun, das er schon lange hatte tun wollen. Er rückte noch ein Stück näher an Britney heran und legte seinen Arm um ihre Schultern. Zu seiner Erleichterung rückte auch sie ihm ein Stück näher. Dann nahm sie seine andere Hand und hielt sie fest. So saßen sie eine lange Zeit, bis es dunkel wurde und sie Mrs Summerfield rufen hörten, dass es Zeit war, ins Bett zu gehen.

Kapitel Sechsundzwanzig –
Goodbye, America ✈

Auf der Fahrt zum Flughafen am nächsten Morgen saß Tobias wieder hinten im Buick und Britney neben ihrem Vater. Mr Summerfield, der sich an die erste Fahrt vom Flughafen nach Appleton erinnert fühlte, versuchte, die beiden in ein Gespräch zu verwickeln, doch weder seiner Tochter noch Tobias waren viele Worte zu entlocken.

Am Flughafen angekommen, trafen sie wieder auf die anderen Austauschteilnehmer. Anna, Björn und Madison winkten schon von der Ferne. Auch sie wirkten etwas bedrückt.

After everybody had checked in their suitcases, it was time to say goodbye. Tobias shook Mr Summerfield's hand. Then Mrs Mayers told him to take care of himself. After that, Madison wished him a safe flight home. Finally, only Britney was left. They looked at each other, both very sad. Then Tobias gave her one last hug. Britney looked around quickly and then, before Tobias realized what was happening, she gave him a little kiss on his lips.

«See you in the summer!» she whispered before she turned around and started walking to where the other Americans were standing.

Bevor Tobias etwas erwidern konnte, hörte er Björns Stimme hinter sich.

«Los, Tobi, wir müssen ans Gate! Frau Berger ist schon ganz ungeduldig!»

Tobias blieb nichts anderes übrig, als den anderen Deutschen zu folgen. Bevor er durch die Passkontrolle ging, drehte er sich noch einmal um. Dort hinten, gleich neben Madison und Mrs Mayers, stand Britney und winkte ihm zu.

Epilogue –
Nachwort ✈

To: Britney Summerfield
From: Tobias Stein
Subject: Wieder in Deutschland

Hello Britney,

I'm back home! The flight was very boring,
but Anna and Björn were sitting next to me
so I always had someone to talk to. (Anna
talked a lot more than Björn and I, of
course.)
I hope that everything is o. k. in Appleton.
Maybe you can e-mail me and tell what is
going on.
I don't like that I can't see you now. Maybe
we can talk on the phone soon. And I'm glad
that you will come here in some months.

Wir sehen uns dann im Sommer.

Tobias

Stefanie Schulz, Jahrgang 1978, studierte Englisch in Göttingen und den USA, bevor sie 2003 Deutschlehrerin an einer amerikanischen Universität wurde. Dieser Job brachte sie auf die Idee, eine deutsch-englische Geschichte zu erzählen. Zurzeit schreibt sie an ihrer Doktorarbeit über amerikanisches Theater.

Daniel Quinlan, geboren 1979 in Chicago, studierte Physik und arbeitete als Lehrer, Übersetzer und DJ in den USA und Deutschland. Seine Koautorin lernte er 2000 auf einem deutsch-amerikanischen Austausch kennen. Seit 2005 ist sein Wohnsitz Göttingen, wo er für seine Doktorarbeit Laser baut.